MW00904070

Introduction
To Christian
Counseling
Theory and Practice

The Rev. Judith Craik, D. Min

Outskirts Press, Inc.
Denver, Colorado

The publisher is not responsible for the views of the author stated herein. The author has represented and warranted full ownership and/or legal right to publish all the materials in this book.

Introduction to Christian Counseling
Theory and Practice
All Rights Reserved.
Copyright © 2009 The Rev. Judith Craik, D. Min
v4.0

This book may not be reproduced, transmitted, or stored in whole or in part by any means, including graphic, electronic, or mechanical without the express written consent of the publisher except in the case of brief quotations embodied in critical articles and reviews.

Outskirts Press, Inc.
http://www.outskirtspress.com

ISBN: 978-1-4327-3861-7

Outskirts Press and the "OP" logo are trademarks belonging to Outskirts Press, Inc.

PRINTED IN THE UNITED STATES OF AMERIC

About the Author

The Rev. Dr. Judith Craik is a pastoral counselor and adjunct professor of counseling at Empire State College in Buffalo, New York. She is a Fellow of the American Association of Pastoral Counselors and a licensed mental health counselor. Dr. Craik is blessed with two sons, two daughters-in-law and two grandchildren.

For

Sheri Landahl

and

my counselees who taught me so much
and enriched my life immeasurably.

Preface

This book is for every Christian who wants to ease the emotional burdens of human beings in pain. If this describes you, then you are probably a good listener and a good friend. People probably seek you out when their lives feel like a mess. And your gift to them is to care about them and listen to their struggles.

You may hope that by learning a little more about "what makes people tick," about what to say and when to say it when people pour out their hearts to you, that you will have a little more confidence in what you do. And that is exactly what this book is designed to do. To give you a little more confidence in your ability to make a difference in the lives of those who already have confidence in your compassion and understanding.

Hopefully, as you read this book you will add some knowledge to your God-given talents. While it is true that sometimes a little bit of knowledge can be a dangerous thing, it is also true that total ignorance is not such a great thing either. A little bit of knowledge with a very large portion of genuine humility can go a long way towards making you a better counselor.

The little bit of knowledge gained from reading this book will consist of a little bit of theory and a great deal of practical application of that theory. You will find the phrase "for example" sprinkled liberally throughout the text. You will also find a line-by-line dialogue between a fictitious counselor and a fictitious counselee to illustrate the concepts of each chapter.

So, do your own thing. Enhance your gifts by learning how to do your own thing better. And remember, the only kind of counselor that can ever make a real difference is the person who recognizes that he or she is simply the vessel of the Holy Spirit - the ultimate healer of human suffering.

Table of Contents

Introduction
First Do No Harm 1
    Fictitious counseling session
    Biblical and theological reflections
    Questions to consider

Chapter I
Where It All Began: Psychoanalytic Theory 17
    Fictitious counseling session
    Biblical and theological reflections
    Questions to consider

Chapter II
From Sex to Relationships: Object Relations 35
    Fictitious counseling sessions
    Biblical and theological reflections
    Questions to consider

Chapter III
Person-Centered Therapy 69
    Fictitious counseling session
    Biblical and theological reflections
    Questions to consider

Chapter IV
Learning To Change 89
     Fictitious counseling sessions
     Biblical and theological reflections
     Questions to consider

Chapter V
Changing How We Think: Cognitive Therapy 113
     Fictitious counseling session
     Biblical and theological reflections
     Questions to consider

Chapter VI
Marriage Counseling..131
     Fictitious counseling sessions
     Biblical and theological reflections
     Questions to consider

Chapter VII
Family Counseling 161
     Fictitious counseling sessions
     Biblical and theological reflections
     Questions to consider

Chapter VIII
Conflict Resolution 185
     Fictitious meetings
     Biblical and theological reflections
     Questions to consider

Chapter IX
Putting It All Together..209
     Fictitious counseling session
     Biblical and theological reflections
     Questions to consider

Subject Index i

Introduction
First Do No Harm

Since you're reading this book, you are probably interested in improving your skills as a Christian counselor. You want to help people and you certainly don't want to hurt them. So here are a few tips that you might use in order to avoid doing harm to a human being in pain. First, you may need to refer some of your counselees to a physician (preferably a psychiatrist) and second, you may need to refer other counselees to a professional counselor.

It really isn't too hard to know when you must refer a counselee to a medical doctor. The American Psychiatric Association (2000) lists the following symptoms exhibited by people who need medications: (1) hallucinations (seeing or hearing things that no one else does), (2) delusions (thoughts that don't fit reality) and/or (3) inappropriate affect (giggling for no apparent reason, for example). You may be able to minister to them, but not until they have received the proper care from a physician.

There are also effective medications for people who don't exhibit these extreme symptoms. People who are depressed and/or very anxious, as well as people who suffer from other mental disorders can also benefit from medications. Depending on the severity of the symptoms, some counselees will want to alleviate their suffering with medications and others will choose not to follow that route. As a counselor, you may want to let your counselees know that medicines are available if they choose to take them.

Fortunately, most of the people who come to you for counseling will not need medical treatment. Among those who may or may not need such care are counselees who suffer from personality disorders. A person who suffers from this type of disorder needs to be referred to a professional counselor.

People with personality disorders are a little harder to recognize than those who must be treated medically. But one way to recognize people with personality disorders is that they are just plain different. Of course, different is good but some people are different in painfully self-defeating ways. Their perceptions of people and events are unrealistic, their emotions are often out of control, they don't get along with other people and they're likely to "fly off the handle" pretty easily (*ibid*). While it is certainly true that some of these symptoms can describe most of us under certain circumstances, someone with a personality disorder fits this description almost all the time. If a counselee has a personality disorder, then the non-professional Christian counselor must refer him or her to a professional mental health provider.

Admittedly, not all professional counselors are equally effective, especially when it comes to treating people with personality disorders. And the fact of the matter is that there are probably some very gifted, well-informed, caring and insightful non-professional counselors who are very effective in their counseling ministries. But the difference between those special non-professionals and a professionally certified counselor is really crucial. That difference is supervision.

In order to be certified as a professional mental health provider, the counselor-in-training must be supervised, often for several years. The reason that supervision is so important is that the supervisor will show the counselor-in-training how his or her own personality affects the therapeutic process. The student counselor will understand that his or her own "baggage" might be really harmful for some counselees but under supervision the student will learn how to avoid causing more harm than good.

Since we all have issues that affect how we relate to other people (*i.e.*, we all have "baggage") supervision is an essential part of the learning experience for all professional counselors. Supervision by a certified supervisor may also be a good idea for the non-professional counselor as well. If you choose to employ a supervisor, that will certainly enhance your ministry of Christian counseling. For short-term counseling, however, supervision is probably not necessary. So how do you know who you can minister to without being supervised and who you must refer to a professional counselor?

Here's the general rule for answering that question. If you have been ministering to someone on a weekly basis for six to eight weeks and there is no discernable difference in that person, then you probably need to make a referral. If the counselee's religious belief system is important to him or her, then someone who is certified by the American Association of Pastoral Counselors (AAPC) is probably the best counselor for that person. Most secular psychologists and social workers are not trained to incorporate a person's faith and beliefs into the therapeutic process. But counselors who are members of AAPC are not only trained to do so but intentional in addressing the counselee's religious as well as his or her emotional well-being.

As a non-professional Christian counselor, you too will want to attend to a counselee's religious (as well as his/her emotional) needs. And you will want to be effective in your ministry. So a good place to start on this journey toward excellence is finding out what *not* to do when someone wants to share his/her burdens with you.

The following verbatim account of a counseling session between a fictitious counselor and a fictitious counselee illustrates some of the things that you should try to avoid doing and saying. See if you can pick out the counselor's mistakes. Then compare your own thoughts with the author's comments, which are presented at the end of the verbatim.

A Fictitious Counseling Session
Showing What Not to Do

Line 1.Gary: Hi, can I talk to you for a few minutes?
Line 2.Counselor: Sure, come in.
Line 3.Gary *(comes in and sits down in a chair across from the*

counselor who sits behind her desk):

Line 4. Counselor: So, how can I help you?

Line 5. Gary: I'm pretty depressed these days. My home life is miserable, I used to enjoy my job but now I'm late every day because I hate to get up and go to work. I'm good at what I do but no one appreciates me. They treat me like I'm stupid.

Line 6. Counselor: Are you stupid?

Line 7. Gary *(shouting):* No, I'm not stupid. But sometimes they treat me like I am.

Line 8. Counselor: What do your colleagues say that makes you feel that way?

Line 9. Gary: Oh, I don't know. It doesn't really matter anyhow because they all hate me. They're jealous of me. They all know I'm so much smarter than they are so they put me down all the time; they sabotage my computer so that it makes mistakes. When I go to the candy machine, I always lose my money. I know someone is doing that on purpose.

Line 10. Counselor: That's awful. The people that you work with sound just awful. I don't know how you can stand it. Have you thought about quitting and finding a better job? Maybe you should just work at home so you don't have to deal with jealous and mean people.

Line 11. Gary *(shouting)*: Find another job? Why should I find another job? They're the ones who should find another job. I've been working at that place for eight years; I've done everything they've asked me to do. All right, sometimes I'm a few hours late but I usually make up the time. I work hard so I take a few hours each day to look at porn on the computer but no one knows so there's no harm done. No way, I'm not looking for another job, let the jerks that are my bosses look for another job.

Line 12. Counselor: You're absolutely right. You shouldn't have to look for another job. It's obvious that you have amazing intelligence that other people would be jealous of. I wish I could do something for you. Would you like me to call your boss and tell him what he's doing to you?

Line 13. Gary *(calmer):* No, that's all right. He probably wouldn't listen to you anyhow.

Line 14. Counselor: I really wouldn't mind doing whatever I

could for you. I'd like to help you if you'll give me a chance.

Line 15. Gary: I wish my wife were as understanding as you are. All she ever does is clean the house and take care of the kids; she never has any time for me.

Line 16. Counselor: How many kids do you have?

Line 17. Gary: I have two, no three kids. The baby is just two months old, I kinda forgot about him. They're good kids I guess. But I feel shut out of the family with my wife taking care of them all the time. What am I, chopped liver? Don't I deserve a little time and attention? If things don't change I'm going to leave the whole bunch of them. Then see how they get along without me.

Line 18. Counselor: Well Gary, I see you in church all the time, and I believe you're a committed Christian so you really can't divorce your wife.

Line 19. Gary *(crying):* But can't you see how miserable I am? I just can't keep on going like this. She has to change.

Line 20. Counselor: You know Gary that none of us has the power to change someone else. But even if she doesn't change, the Bible is very clear that you cannot divorce your wife.

Line 21. Gary: Well, I have friends who tell me that if I'm so unhappy that I should divorce her. One friend in particular really understands me and it feels so good to be really understood.

Line 22. Counselor: Regardless of what your friends tell you, the teaching of scripture is very clear. Luke Chapter 16 and verse 18 'Anyone who divorces his wife and marries another woman commits adultery.' I'm just trying to get you to live up to your faith. Well, it's clear to me that we need to talk again. I have a meeting that I must go to, so can we meet again tomorrow at the same time? In the meantime, let me give you a hug, you seem to need it.

Analysis

Line 1. From the very beginning, Gary is very clear about what he wants from the counselor. He didn't say "can we talk" he asked if he could talk to her, and by implication, he wants her to listen to him. But the dialogue that follows indicates that Gary's stated need was not met. That is, the counselor did not listen very well.

Line 2. The counselor's response is appropriate, except that she should have made her time limitations clear at the beginning of the conversation. Gary could have assumed that the counselor was not very interested in him and his problems when she rather abruptly ended the counseling session (line 22).

Line 3. When the counselor sits behind her desk, she is unwittingly sending the wrong message, which is that she is the person with authority and therefore the one with more power. The counselee may then feel like a student sitting in front of the school principal and would be more inclined to be defensive than to engage in an open and honest conversation.

Line 4. The counselor begins by asking Gary how she can help him. There are two problems with this simple question. First, the counselor assumes that Gary wants to be helped (which is not what he asked for). Second, she assigns to herself the position of helper, which only increases her authority and the power associated with that authority.[1]

Line 5. Gary is saying that he is troubled emotionally ("I'm depressed") and that his relationships are unsatisfactory ("no one appreciates me"). He also seems quite irresponsible. Because he hates his job he seems to think that he's entitled to come to work late.

Gary talks about several different problems so the counselor should have simply encouraged Gary to say more. That way he decides what the session will be about.

Line 6. When the counselor asked this question she may have wanted Gary to affirm that he is not stupid. But the question is manipulative. It is intended to elicit a particular response rather than provide information that the counselor believes would be helpful.

Line 7. Gary has been "led down the garden path" and he is angry. Does he feel like he's been manipulated? Or did he expect that the counselor would have been more supportive by assuring

_____

[1] The helper has something that the "helpee" needs. So the "helpee" is willing to submit to the helper in order to get. When the "helpee" submits to the helper, that gives the helper more power.

him that he is not stupid? Either way, Gary's response indicates that he is emotionally volatile. He "flies off the handle" very easily.

Line 8. The counselor should not have asked Gary to repeat accusations that are obviously painful for him. She may have been curious about what his colleagues say, but satisfying her curiosity is not going to help Gary. Or, maybe she believes that by talking about the criticisms, that is, once he "gets it out" he'll feel better. This is a common mistake in timing. Talking about painful events before the counselee is ready to do so can cause more harm than good.

Line 9. Gary reveals that he really does have a serious personality disorder. He assumes that he knows what other people are thinking (a cognitive distortion), he is also paranoid in his belief that others would sabotage his computer and underscores that paranoia when he insists that someone is preventing him from getting candy from a machine.

Line 10. At this point, the counselor should have kindly told Gary that it sounds as if he really is in more pain than she has the experience to deal with. Instead, she reinforces his paranoia. It may be that Gary wanted some reassurance about his unrealistic belief that everyone was out to get him, but to gratify that need only reinforces and prolongs his paranoia.

The counselor then goes on to give Gary some advice - a common mistake. Gary didn't ask to talk to the counselor so that she could give him advice; he just wants her to listen to him.

Line 11. Gary continues to reveal that he is seriously disturbed. His anger is out of control, he believes that all of his problems are caused by other people, he does not seem to realize that he is responsible for his own behavior, his sense of morality is immature (everything is acceptable if no one catches him) and he may have some sexual problems.

Line 12. The counselor was wise not to call attention to Gary's inappropriate behaviors and attitudes. He does not seem to be capable of being honest about himself and would probably have heard her comments as criticisms. If Gary believed that he was being criticized, then that would almost certainly have closed the door for the possibility of ministry to him.

But the counselor did make several mistakes. First, she should not have agreed with Gary about his perceptions of others. That only reinforces his pathology. Also, she should not have offered to call Gary's boss. She seems to have adopted the role of a "mommy" who would "fix it and make it all better." As a result, Gary doesn't need to be responsible for his own well-being. He can act like an irresponsible child.

In addition, the counselor was about to betray Gary's legitimate expectation that what he says to the counselor would be kept confidential. If she had called Gary's boss, she would have divulged the fact that Gary was talking about him.

Line 13. Gary calms down. Apparently he got what he wanted from his counselor, someone to take responsibility for him, to treat him like a child and try to make him feel better. The problem is that making Gary feel better is not going to help him. Making Gary feel better only takes away the need for him to see himself (instead of everyone else) as his own worst enemy.[2] Why should *he* change if his unhappiness is everyone else's fault?

Line 14. Again, the counselor insists that she wants to help Gary by fixing his problems. This time, she reverses the relationship between counselor and counselee. The counselor wants Gary to "give her a chance" to help him. Her need to be helpful has replaced Gary's need to just talk to someone.

Line 15. Gary is much too self-absorbed to respond to the counselor's need to be helpful. His self-absorption is evident in his complaint about his wife, who "never has time" for him. The counselor may take Gary's affirmation of her as a compliment, but it says a lot more about Gary's emotional needs than about her competence as a Christian counselor.

Line 16. Gary has clearly indicated that he and his wife are having problems. But the counselor responds by asking for information that is not directly related to the marriage. This unfortunately, is a common mistake. This is not to say that

---

[2] One of the differences between counselors and friends is that friends cheer each other up while counselors try to remove roadblocks to the healing power of the Holy Spirit. Feeling better is a short-term experience, healing can be for a lifetime.

counselors don't require information about a counselee. But the amount of information that is acquired may be inversely related to the value of the counseling session. The counselee is a human being whose actual presence can be experienced by the counselor. That personal connection is much more important than facts about the counselee's life.

Line 17. Again, Gary's self-absorption is only too evident. He forgets how many children he has, he longs to be treated like a child himself and then states what was probably his previously decided-upon solution, which is to leave his wife and children.

Line 18. The counselor picks up on Gary's now not-so-secret solution. But instead of discussing Gary's feelings and his misperceptions she launches into her own agenda. The counselor is opposed to divorce, and imposes her opposition on Gary by appealing to his faith.

Gary's agenda seems to be to have someone (1) listen to his complaints about his family and his co-workers and (2) give him permission to leave his family because he is so unhappy. He also seems to be looking for (3) someone who will take care of him. The Christian counselor decided that her agenda was to: (1) affirm Gary's unhealthy perceptions of himself and others, (2) try to make him feel better and (3) prevent him from divorcing his wife. (The issue of divorce will be discussed more fully in Chapter VI.)

The counselor's first two goals served only to prevent Gary from getting the help that he needed. They also kept him in a state of extreme self-absorption and childish irresponsibility. The counselor's third goal was a direct contradiction to Gary's desire for a divorce and highly unlikely to be even considered by Gary. The counselor and the counselee each had his and her own agenda. The result was that they never really communicated with each other.

Line 19. Gary is well aware of his own pain but cannot see that he might be at least part of the problem. It is his wife who needs to change, according to Gary, not he.

Line 20. The counselor correctly challenges Gary and teaches him that the reality is that one person cannot change another. But that doesn't prevent her from trying to change Gary's mind about divorcing his wife.

Line 21. Here we have a good example of Gary's thinking from what he is *not* saying. The clues come from what he *is* saying. He has a special friend who "really understands" him. It may be assumed that this friend is the woman for whom Gary would like to leave his wife.

Line 22. But the counselor misses what Gary only implied. She is so intent on pushing her own agenda that she fails to respond to the reason that Gary wants a divorce. He apparently wants a more nurturing, comforting and available "mommy." Unfortunately, that is exactly the role that the counselor plays when she gives Gary a hug. The counselor ends the session by affirming Gary's dysfunctional and self-defeating needs.

Hopefully, this fictitious account has adequately illustrated some of the things that the Christian counselor ought not to do. In the following chapters, verbatim accounts of counseling sessions will illustrate some of the things that the effective Christian counselor should do.

Biblical and Theological Reflections

The counseling session presented above included many mistakes on the part of the fictitious counselor. What does scripture have to teach us about her mistakes? First and foremost, we saw that Christians, especially Christian counselors must be humble. The counselor should have had enough humility to recognize that Gary's issues were too pervasive and complex. That is, Gary would not be able to relate to the counselor in a healing way. But the counselor seems to have been too proud to admit that she could not minister effectively to him and as a result she failed to make an appropriate referral.

The fact of the matter is, that no counselor would have been able to minister effectively to Gary in just one session. However, if the Christian counselor had complied with Gary's original request and had just listened to him, then Gary might have listened to her if she had referred him to a professional counselor.

The counselor's lack of humility may also be the reason that she failed to take into account the imbalance of power between herself and the person she wanted to help. When the counselor sat behind her desk she let it be known that she is the one who is the authority and therefore has more power. That is not only detrimental to the therapeutic relationship; it flies in the face of biblical teaching.

When the devil offered Jesus "all the authority and splendor" of the kingdoms of the world if Jesus would worship him, Jesus refused to do so (Luke 4:5-8). Jesus had no need for power and authority from the devil because He already had them. Jesus' power came from His relationship with the Father. The Christian counselor's spiritual power must come from the same source. It should not come by flaunting our "exalted" positions as counselors.

Another one of the counselor's mistakes was to treat Gary like a child. She assumed responsibility for his well-being, tried to comfort him as if he was a child and even physically nurtured him like she would a child. But despite Gary's emotional immaturity, he is not a child and treating him like he is one only keeps him in his very immature state. To be sure, Jesus held up child-like faith as an example of the kind of trust that is needed for one to enter the kingdom of heaven. But He certainly did not suggest that we should become childish, only child-like in our faith in God (Matthew 18:2 - 4).

The goal of counseling is not to encourage a counselee to remain in an immature stage of development. Indeed, the goal of counseling and of life itself is to encourage growth and development so that human beings can meet the challenges that life throws at us. Adults who think and behave like children are not equipped to handle the responsibilities and tragedies of life. The Christian counselor who treats an adult as if he/she is a child is actually preventing that person from dealing effectively with his/her own life.

The fictitious counselor also revealed a pharisaical attitude about the solution to Gary's problems. She insisted that he must not divorce his wife and quoted scripture in order to prove that she was right. The problem is that she completely ignored Gary's reason for divorcing his wife, which is his painful longing for a "mommy" who would take care of him.

The counselor substituted the letter of the law for the principle of the law, which is to love our neighbors as ourselves. The counselor would have been much more effective if she had attended to Gary's emotional suffering than she was by quoting the law. She should have simply acknowledged, with neither approval nor condemnation, Gary's need for attention, for nurturing and respect. If she had done that, then Gary would have felt known and accepted by the counselor. As a result he may have been much more inclined to listen to what she had to say.

This Christian counselor was not only pharisaical in her responses to Gary; the timing of those responses was terrible. Gary was obviously distraught. He was so unhappy that he opened himself to a relative stranger whom he hoped might just listen to him and possibly even share his pain.

When a person is suffering that is definitely not the time to argue with him or her. Again, Jesus is the example for us to follow. When the Canaanite woman came to Jesus pleading with Him to heal her daughter, His disciples wanted Him to turn her away. He told the woman that He had come for "the lost sheep of Israel" (Matthew 15:24). Yet, He saw her suffering and honored her faith. Jesus stated His mission but would not kick her when she was down. He did not argue with her, He healed her (Matthew 15: 21-28). The Christian counselor believed that divorce was wrong. But unlike Jesus, she argued with a human being in pain and in doing so failed to be a vessel of God's grace.

This is not to suggest that scriptural truths about divorce or any other topic have no place in Christian counseling. But how the Bible is used is the important factor here. While the prophetic preacher will certainly tell his/her congregation truths from scripture that will be hard for them to hear, in the counseling session with a vulnerable human being in pain, the situation is very different. There is a time to afflict the comfortable and a time to comfort the afflicted. Counseling is usually the latter.

The counselor who uses specific Bible verses to get the counselee to obey him or her is using scripture inappropriately. It is the message of the Bible as a whole that must be incorporated into the counseling process by a counselor who has made that message a part of his or her soul. Then the Holy Spirit will use that message and work through the counselor to affect a measure of healing in a suffering human being.[3] Scripture can certainly be quoted in order to teach, to comfort and even admonish. But it should never be used as a means to coerce compliance with the counselor's beliefs.

Another mistake made by the counselor was her attempt to solve Gary's problems by trying to change him. She tried to make him feel better about himself as well as change his views about divorce. It is never the counselor who changes a counselee in any meaningful way. Real change is accomplished when a human being, by the grace of God, allows the Holy Spirit to work in his or her mind and heart. The counselor can remove the roadblocks to God's work but for the most part, that is usually the limit of his/her counseling ministry.

This belief, that it is not the counselor who heals but God, is a theological understanding based on scripture. When Jesus sent out the twelve disciples to minister to the house of Israel (Matthew 10: 1-42) he told them that those who receive them also receive Him. The disciples represented Jesus. And as His representatives, Jesus empowered them to heal. When their ministry was successful it was because of Jesus' power not their own.

Like those early disciples, we too are ambassadors for Christ. Our power to heal does not come from our own special gifts or theoretical understandings or positions of authority; it comes from God. We are simply the vessels of that power. But sometimes even God's power is thwarted by the free will of people in pain. That is, sometimes human beings put up roadblocks to God's healing power.

A roadblock to the work of the Holy Spirit is anything that prevents a human being from receiving the grace of God. That grace is always available to us but we fail to receive it for as many reasons as there are people in pain.

Let us look at Gary's roadblocks. First, he does not recognize that he needs to be healed. If Gary does not acknowledge that his behaviors and way of thinking are self-defeating, then he will not

---

[3] The author's theology of healing is clearly evident here. It will be explained more fully in the final chapter of the book. The reader is encouraged to define his or her own understanding of God's part in the healing process.

realize that he needs God's help. In addition, if he fails to acknowledge his own sinful behavior, then he has no reason to ask for forgiveness. Gary's failure to take responsibility for his own behavior and his failure to acknowledge his sin prevent him from recognizing that he needs to be both forgiven and healed. These failures become roadblocks to receiving God's grace - the healing power of the Holy Spirit.

The fact is that Gary may not even be aware that he is doing anything wrong when, for example, he watches pornography. He hasn't been caught so, according to him, it must be all right to watch it. Apparently he thinks like a small child. If he doesn't get punished, then he hasn't been bad (Kohlberg, 1964). His immature morality is a roadblock to the healing power of the Hoy Spirit because he doesn't know that he needs to be forgiven and is therefore unable to receive God's grace.

Understanding Gary's immature moral development gives the Christian counselor a good alternative to simply admonishing him to stop sinning. Helping Gary acknowledge and understand why his humanity is expressed in the way that it is would probably be far more effective than simply telling him to stop being who he is.

In addition to Gary's delayed moral development, he is in pain. He is willing to divorce his wife and leave his children because he is desperate for someone to nurture him, and apparently his "friend" is willing to do exactly that. Gary's need is so great and the pain of not having that need met is so hard for him to bear that he is willing to destroy his family in order to alleviate his suffering. He thinks that his "friend" can make him feel better so he doesn't allow God to heal him.

Another roadblock to the work of the Holy Spirit is Gary's loss of faith. Even though Gary went to a Christian counselor and attends church regularly, there is no indication that God is a significant part of his life. His emotional suffering is so intense that he apparently no longer has faith in a God who loves him and is ready to heal him. Some people do turn to God when their lives are filled with pain. But Gary is so severely damaged[4] that he cannot experience the

---

[4] This is evidenced by his extreme self-absorption, his sense of entitlement, his paranoia, his emotional volatility, his troubled relationships, etc.

presence of God. He longs for a physically present "mommy" not a Father in Heaven. His lack of faith prevents him from wanting God to heal him, which is another roadblock to the power of God in his life.

So what does this suggest about the ministry of Christian counseling? It is the author's belief that the Christian counselor can be most effective by removing the roadblocks to the counselee's capacity to receive the Comforter who pours out on a suffering human being the healing power of God. The counselor can be the vessel of the Holy Spirit as he/she removes those roadblocks but it is God who does the healing.

Questions to Consider

1) Are you clear about why you want to be a Christian counselor? Do you have an inordinate need to make people feel better? Do you have a tendency to be everyone's "mother"? Do you enjoy the feeling of superiority that comes when other people trust your advice and counsel?

2) Many Christians engage in informal counseling on a regular basis. Do your friends call you on the phone just to talk, do your neighbors stop by in order to tell you what is going on in their lives? If so, then you are already a Christian counselor. Can you use what you learn from this chapter in these informal settings?

3) Looking back on recent encounters with people who tell you that they "just want to talk to you," what has been your typical response? Do you mostly listen, do you give advice, are you judgmental, have you ever repeated something that may have been meant for you alone?

4) What is your theological understanding of God's healing power? Does God heal against a person's free will? Does healing take place only through scripture?

REFERENCES

American Psychiatric Association (2000). *Diagnostic and statistical manual IV - R.* Arlington, VA: American Psychiatric Association.

……….. *Holy Bible: New International Version* (1984). East Brunswick, NJ: International Bible Society.

Kohlberg, L. (1964). Development of moral character and moral ideology. In M. Hoffman and L. Hoffman (eds.) *Review of child development research* (Vol. 1). New York: Russell Sage Foundation.

SUGGESTED READINGS

Cooper, A. (1989). Concepts of therapeutic effectiveness in psychoanalysis: A historical review. *Psychoanalytic Inquiry,* 9(1) pp. 4-25.

Frank, J. D. and Frank, J. B. (1991). *Persuasion and Healing.* Baltimore: Johns Hopkins University Press.

Garfield, A. and Bergin, A. (1992). *Handbook of psychotherapy and behavior change.* New York: Wiley.

CHAPTER I
Where It All Began:
Psychoanalytic Theory

When we think of counseling, we envision two or more people talking to each other about problems in the life of one of them. The founding father of this kind of counseling (sometimes called talk therapy) was Sigmund Freud. If you know anything about Freud, you may be tempted to skip this chapter - but don't. Yes, he was extremely antagonist toward religion in general and Christianity in particular. Much of what he taught has since been shown to be woefully lacking in verifiable evidence and some of his ideas about human nature are probably just plain wrong. But some of his concepts have been validated and most of his techniques are still in use today. So, "don't throw the baby out with the bathwater."

Given the significant problems with Freudian theory, only a few of his suggestions need be considered. This chapter will describe some of Freud's most widely used concepts and then show how they can be used in counseling, including Christian counseling.

Specifically, the four most important contributions of Freud's Psychodynamic Theory[5] to the counseling endeavor are: An understanding of; (1) the unconscious, (2) transference, (3) interpretation and (4) resistance. Each of these will be described in some detail so that the Christian counselor may use them for the

---

[5] The theory is known as psychodynamic, its practice is psychoanalysis.

benefit of those to whom he or she seeks to minister.

Perhaps the most well known of Freud's teachings is his understanding of the unconscious. One way to understand this concept is to think of it as a storage bin for all the thoughts and motivations that are out of the awareness of the individual. For example, sometimes bad news may be so painful that we are just not capable of accepting that information, so we temporarily put it in the unconscious. When one hears of the sudden death of a loved one, for example, that information may be ignored, that is put in the unconscious, until the hearer is ready to accept it.

A much more common example of how we use the unconscious is what is known as motivated forgetting. The following story is an example of this unconscious motivation. "Horace" (not a real person)[6] failed to sign his check to the U.S. Treasury when he sent in his tax forms. He consciously wanted to meet his obligation as a citizen to pay his taxes. But he had an unconscious desire to keep his hard earned money for himself. So Horace filled out the forms and made out a check, but he "forgot" to sign it.

Well, anyone can forget but why are we more likely to forget something that we really didn't want to do in the first place? Freud would say, and most people would agree, that (as was the case with Horace) we want to forget but we don't want to know that we want to forget so our "forgetfulness" becomes unconscious.

Unconscious thoughts and events can influence what we do and how we feel. But forgetting to sign a check will probably have few if any lasting psychological effects. There are times, however, when putting material into the unconscious can have horrendous consequences.

Within the last five to ten years we have all heard about the condition known as Post Traumatic Stress Disorder. Initially we heard about it as it applied to men and women who as children, experienced sexual abuse, sometimes at the hands of a trusted relative or even a clergyman. Typically, these men and women did not talk about their experiences until many years after they

---

[6] All of the names used in the text are fictitious, except of course the names of the authors whose works are cited.

happened. Why?

In most cases the painful experiences were "buried" in the unconscious, they were "forgotten" because they evoked such painful feelings of shame and betrayal. But as the abused children grew to maturity, these unconscious events began to affect their lives. Some turned to alcohol and/or drugs (Herman, 1992) in order to keep the experiences out of their awareness and buried in the unconscious. Some became sexually promiscuous (*ibid*) because they believed that they were bad people even though they were unaware that this feeling of being bad came from what someone else had done to them.More typically, people became extremely distressed during sexual encounters with their spouses and could not understand why. Adults who had been molested during childhood felt ashamed and betrayed, they experienced rage and impotence but the events that caused these feelings were out of their own awareness, they were unconscious.

As this tragic example suggests, the pain that is associated with "forgotten" events often increases in intensity as the child who experienced them grows to maturity. Conscious, remembered events can also evoke painful feelings. Every time a person remembers a bitter argument, every time someone remembers a humiliating experience, the feelings associated with those events may grow in intensity. Unconscious material has the same effect even though the cause of the feelings is no longer conscious.

It would be a mistake, however, to assume that traumatic events are the only ones that become unconscious. Most of us do not suffer from severe traumas experienced during childhood but we all have events, motivations and thoughts of which we are not aware. We can understand why traumatic events are repressed in the unconscious; but why do we hide from everyday experiences by keeping them out of our own awareness, that is, in the unconscious?

First, we keep painful thoughts and events in the unconscious because we are inadvertently taught to do so. This is especially true of events (including words) that evoke anger. Our culture, through our parents, teaches us that it is bad to be angry. But anger is a natural physiological response to pain, both physical and emotional. And we have all experienced painful events. Words such as "can't you do anything right" certainly cause pain. So we repress these hurtful words into the unconscious because we don't want to experience the anger that they evoke in us. And we keep them in the unconscious because we have been taught that feeling angry is "bad."

The second reason for keeping events and motives in the unconscious is a need to be in control of ourselves. Strong emotions threaten to overwhelm us. We are afraid of being controlled by them instead of by our own capacity for rational thought. We may feel a murderous rage toward someone but rationally we know that the consequences of acting on that rage could be catastrophic. So the events that resulted in a feeling of rage remain in the unconscious and the rage associated with them *seems* less threatening. Of course, the rage may burst out at the most inopportune times and toward the wrong person. While the cause of the rage is out of our conscious awareness, the rage itself may still be present.

One way of dealing with painful events that are caused by a significant person in our lives, especially a parent, is to unconsciously transfer the hurtful/angry relationship with the parent on to someone else. This process was discovered by Sigmund Freud and is one of his most significant and insightful concepts (Freud, 1969). He called this process transference.

Freud found that his patients would often treat him as if he was an important figure in the patient's life, usually the patient's mother. Obviously as a man, Freud did not resemble the patient's mother, but the counselee treated him as if he was just like her mother. Initially, this concept was met with derision by other doctors. But we cannot easily dismiss the concept of transference because we have seen it too often, not only in counseling sessions but also in every-day life.

For example, "Stella" (a fictitious person) felt rejected by a cold and distant father. Stella's feelings of rejection were so painful for her that she put the cause of those feelings in her unconscious. Even though the cause was unconscious, Stella knew that she was bitterly angry at her father.[7]

---

[7] In counseling, Stella may give reasons for the way she feels about her father

Many years after she left home, Stella married "Reginald" (also a fictitious person) who loves and accepts her. But over time, Stella treats Reginald the same way she treated her father, with anger and hostility. Reginald has not changed but Stella has transferred the feelings that she had for her father on to her husband. Of course, the reason that Stella treated Reginald as if he was her father is unconscious. She is completely unaware that she relates to a warm and loving husband as if he is her cold and distant father.

What may not be clear is the reason that an adult relates to someone who stands in for the parent long after the adult has left home. To say that old habits die-hard is partly true but fails to fully explain why we transfer our relationship with a parent to another person later in life.

Freud's explanation is that we seek to replicate an earlier relationship in order to repair it. Of course, it would make more sense to repair a conflicted relationship with a rejecting father with him, not with a husband. But who ever said that human behavior always makes sense? Since the cause of the conflict is unconscious, the relationship is replayed over and over again with different people. Unless the person who has a conflicted relationship with a parent recognizes that such is the case, he or she will also repeat that relationship with the counselor.

For example, a counselor might say to a counselee (we'll call her "Tina") that she seems very nervous, to which Tina responds "I really resent you being so critical of me." Assuming that the counselor had not meant to be critical, the counselor might conclude from this that Tina, without being consciously aware of it, is angry with her mother who was perceived to be overly critical. Tina has transferred her relationship with her mother on to the counselor. So what should the counselor do about this transference?

When transference happens in a counseling session, the counselor must recognize it as transference and not assume that he is the problem. But telling the counselee that she is actually

---

that don't seem to fit the intensity of her feelings. The real reason for her anger is unconscious.

relating to him as if he was someone else may not be the answer either. Rather, the information that the counselor gains from the transference simply provides an important clue about the counselee's relationship with a parent. Later, when the counselee is actually talking more directly about that parent, the counselor has information about which the counselee is probably unaware. What to do with that information requires some discussion about interpretation.

Knowing about the unconscious and about transference is useful, but it doesn't give the Christian counselor a clue about how to respond to those who want you to listen to their stories and their heartaches. Whatever the counselor says when he/she responds to a counselee is an interpretation. Before describing the relevant factors of effective interpretations, it is important to examine some of the basic assumptions related to this important concept.

The first assumption is that interpretations enable a counselee to achieve a deeper understanding of himself or herself. Related to this first assumption is the second, which is that with deeper understanding and a motivation to change comes the ability to gain appropriate control over one's life and greater satisfaction with one's relationships.

Many people have found that a relevant interpretation offered in a grace-filled way and taking place in a trusting relationship does give a person greater self-understanding. The counselee may find this new level of understanding to be liberating. The truth about ourselves can make us free from the unconscious events and thoughts that drive us in self-defeating ways.

This leads to the second assumption about the efficacy of interpretation. That is, once a person discovers the truth about herself she can change her reactions to the now-conscious motives that had previously plagued her. Truth may be liberating but without the motivation to change, there is little hope for healing. The Christian counselor can rest in the knowledge that the Holy Spirit offers not only motivation to change but also the power to do so. Interpreting the unconscious can take away the roadblocks to the power of God who works in the life of a counselee.

But those interpretations must be both timely and verifiable. The timing of the counselor's interpretation is actually dictated by the counselee. An insight offered before it is ready to be heard will fall on deaf ears. The example cited earlier in which a counselee (Tina) transferred her relationship with a critical mother on to the counselor provides a good example about when to offer an interpretation. When Tina speaks about her mother she may begin to feel very angry. The effective counselor will wait until she is talking about her mother and is ready to acknowledge her anger with her before he interprets the unconscious reasons for her anger - that she was perceived by Tina to be painfully critical.

In addition to offering interpretations at the right moment, they should also be verifiable. That is, the counselor should be able to give a reason for why he believes that his interpretation is correct. This is best done by using the counselee's own words. For example, "Marianne" says that she is sick and tired of picking up after her husband, to which the counselor might respond "you're angry with him." If Marianne asks what makes him think that, the counselor need only repeat her words she's "sick and tired…"Verifiable interpretations will avoid the mistake of going deeper into the unconscious than the counselee is ready for. It is not necessary to actually offer verification, but the counselor should be mindful of the reason for his interpretation when he makes one.

As this example illustrates, interpretations should be like a mirror reflecting back to the counselee what she might not be able to see about herself. This does not mean that the counselor should act like the mirror in the story of Sleeping Beauty that tells the queen that she is the fairest of them all. The counselor does not respond by telling the counselee what she wants to hear, he interprets what the counselee is saying and feeling.

For example, when an attractive woman says to a counselor that she knows that she is not very pretty, the counselor doesn't try to convince her that she is pretty, even though she may want him to do so. The counselor reflects back to the counselee her belief and the emotions that go with it. He might say that she seems very sad about not being pretty, or ask how she feels about not being pretty. The counselor acknowledges the counselee's feelings and in so doing, the counselee can then decide if she wants to deal with her self-perception (or her search for a compliment) in order to mitigate her painful feelings.

As this example indicates, there is an important difference between interpretation and encouragement or advice or guidance or rules to follow or scripture to be obeyed. As the word implies, interpretation is like reading between the lines of a book. In the counseling endeavor, the book is an autobiography. The counselee is the author of the book that the counselor is reading. The reader interprets the author's meaning but the author is the final authority on the reader's interpretations. Since the reader can never be sure that his interpretations of the book are correct, asking a question of the author is often the best interpretation.

There will be times, however, when an interpretation is correct but the counselee will either deny that it is correct or seem to ignore it. When that happens the counselee may be resisting the counselor's interpretation. This resistance takes place for a very good reason (Freud, 1969).

One of the most frustrating aspects of counseling for the inexperienced counselor is the counselee's apparent refusal to hear what the counselor has said. The counselor may repeat the same thing several times on different occasions only to have the counselee seem to change the subject. This is called resistance, which can be seen as stubbornness or, more appropriately as an important clue to the counselee's fears and vulnerabilities.

When a counselee does not seem to hear an interpretation it may be because the interpretation touches on something in the counselee that is too painful for her to acknowledge. To try to force the counselee to hear and respond to the interpretation is not only ineffective but also potentially dangerous. If the counselee is pushed into accepting something before she is ready, the result could be severely heightened anxiety or even a serious decompensation - what is commonly called a nervous breakdown. It may be frustrating when a counselor feels that the counselee is ignoring him, but it is crucial to remember that the counselee will accept an interpretation when or if she is psychologically ready to do so - and not before then.

For example, "Todd" seems very anxious when he talks about his mother's closet. But when the counselor says "you seem nervous about your mother's closet" Todd goes on to talk about a large wooden spoon that his mother always kept on the kitchen counter. He seems to have ignored the counselor's interpretation. But he hasn't, he's resisting it. It may be that both the closet and the spoon were used to punish Todd so the two are associated with pain. But it is only the memory of spending hours alone shut up in his mother's closet that is unconscious. The spoon is less painful to remember so Todd talks about what is conscious. In this example, the effective counselor will follow the counselee and not try to talk about the more painful subject of the instrument of punishment that was his mother's closet.

The basic practice of counseling that follows the psychoanalytic model, then, is offering interpretations in order to make conscious that which had been unconscious. Sometimes the counselor will interpret transference but more often the counselor will simply read between the lines of the counselee's autobiography. When resistance is encountered, the counselor will always recognize that what seems like stubbornness is actually an essential part of maintaining the counselee's self-cohesion. The following record of a fictitious counseling session will illustrate most of these basic concepts. (Transference will be illustrated in the next chapter.)

A Fictitious Counseling Session

Frank is in his early fifties, married with two children both of whom are in college. He is a business manager at a local tire store and an active member of his local congregation. His wife called the pastor to make an appointment for Frank so that he could talk to her about his insomnia.

Line 1. Frank: Hi, are you busy?

Line 2. Counselor: Oh, hi Frank. I'm on the phone. I'll be with you in just a few minutes. *(A few minutes later).* I'm sorry to keep you waiting Frank. Please come in.

Line 3. Frank: Sorry to bother you, but Susan thought it might help if I talked to someone.

Line 4. Counselor: You are definitely not bothering me, Frank.

What did you want to talk about?

Line 5. Frank: Well, I'm dead tired all the time, I just can't fall asleep. I'm cranky, I can't concentrate at work. My life just seems to be going down the tubes.

Line 6. Counselor: I'm really sorry to hear that, Frank. Have you any idea what's keeping you awake at night?

Line 7. Frank: I don't know, I go to bed and it's like my mind just won't stop going.

Line 8. Counselor: What's going through your mind when it doesn't shut off?

Line 9. Frank: Well, I guess it's mostly work stuff. And I think about my mother a lot. She died about two years ago and I really miss her.

Line 10. Counselor: How long have you been having trouble falling asleep?

Line 11. Frank *(laughing)*: Well, now that I think about it, around two years, around the time that mom died. Do you think that could have something to do with it?

Line 12. Counselor: Well, I don't know, tell me about you and your mom.

Line 13. Frank: Oh, she was a great lady. Everyone loved her, she was great with my kids. She used to be a nurse and a lot of the people she took care of came to the funeral. There were so many people there, I didn't even know most of them.

Line 14. Counselor: She sounds like a wonderful woman. Did you and she have a good relationship?

Line 15. Frank: There were so many people there that they had to bring in extra chairs, even then a lot of people had to stand. *(Long pause)*. I'm sorry, what did you say?

Line 16. Counselor: I asked about your relationship with your mother.

Line 17. Frank: Well, I wasn't a very good son, I didn't see her much after I left for college. You know how it is. You get busy, things come up. She was a very independent woman, she never asked for much from me. And I never needed much from her. *(Long pause)*. I guess she was a good mother. She always worked and there were five of us kids. I guess I just learned to take care of myself.

Line 18. Counselor: She was a good woman but a little lacking as a mother.

Line 19. Frank: *(Weeping)*. The truth is, I hated her. She was never there for me. She was a selfish bitch who only cared about taking care of strangers. She never cared at all about her own kids. *(Long pause)*.

Line 20. Counselor: That was really hard for you to admit to yourself.

Line 21. Frank: You're not supposed to say bad things about your mother, especially when she's dead. But now that the truth is out, I have to tell you it feels like a very heavy burden has been lifted off my shoulders.

Line 22. Counselor: I'm glad to hear that. I hope you'll feel free to give me a call when you want to talk some more.

Analysis

Line 1. Frank is early for a pre-arranged appointment.

Line 2. The counselor is mindful of Frank's discomfort but does not cut her telephone conversation short. Keeping appropriate boundaries is essential, and time is one of those boundaries.

Line 3. Frank is reluctant to admit that he needs help. He implies that he is coming for his wife's sake.

Line 4. The counselor wisely avoids Frank's implication that his wife is the one with a problem. Frank is the person sitting in her office, not his wife, so he is the focus of attention.

Line 5. Frank describes the symptoms but doesn't speculate about what may cause his sleeplessness. Since his sleep disturbance has affected his life quite dramatically, it is a little unusual that he has not at least taken some guesses about the causes of his insomnia. Does he lack insight, or does he not want to know what is causing him so much distress?

Line 6. The counselor probes Frank's capacity for insight.

Line 7. Frank avoids the question about the possible cause by describing his symptoms. Is this resistance?

Line 8. Now the counselor is more specific. She invites Frank to talk about problems that might be troubling him and keeping him up at night. She isn't sure if he is avoiding the cause of his sleeplessness or just focused on the symptoms.

Line 9. Frank offers two possible causes, work and the death of his mother. The fact that he mentions work before he talks about the death of his mother may be an indication that he would rather focus on the less painful issue.

Line 10. This question is more than a search for information. Work related stress is often experienced as anxiety, which can cause insomnia. But the counselor takes a guess that it is the loss of his mother that is causing Frank's distress.

Line 11. Frank's laughter suggests embarrassment. This is a common reaction when someone has been "found out," that is, when the unconscious has been made conscious. Frank seems to be close to realizing that his sleep disturbance has something to do with the loss of his mother.

Line 12. The counselor has guessed that grief over the loss of Frank's mother is the cause of his sleep disturbances, but she doesn't know for sure. She could have verified her guess by pointing to Frank's embarrassed laughter, but that probably wouldn't seem like much of a verification to Frank.

Line 13. Frank avoids the counselor's request to tell her about his relationship with his mother. Instead, he talks about her funeral and how *other people* felt about her.

Line 14. The counselor is mindful of Frank's resistance to talking about his relationship with his mother but his response in line 11 ("Do you think that could have something to do with it"?) suggests that he wants to deal with the unconscious thoughts that are troubling him. So the counselor offers two possible directions, which gives Frank a choice about which one he wants to pursue. First, she repeats Frank's statements that his mother was a wonderful person so that he could continue to talk about how other people felt about her. Then she asked about Frank's relationship with his mother.

Line 15. Initially Frank chooses the less painful path and continues to talk about how other people felt about his mother. But after several minutes of silence, Frank decides to pursue what he had previously resisted.

Line 16. The counselor had respected Frank's earlier need to resist talking about how he felt about his mother but now that he seems ready to talk about it, she repeats her earlier question.

Line 17. Frank takes the blame for a less than satisfying relationship with his mother. It is difficult to be critical of his now-deceased mother so he avoids doing so by being critical of himself. But then he gives an important hint about her role as mother when he says "I never needed much from her." He seems to have surprised himself by this admission and is now less sure that his mother was all that he needed her to be. He only "guesses" that she was a good mother and then continues to defend her.

Line 18. The counselor's interpretation that Frank's mother was "lacking" was a cautious one. Frank had simply said that he never needed much from her, which the counselor interpreted as Frank's way to cope with a mother who was not sufficiently present emotionally and/or physically to meet his needs.

Line 19. Now Frank is fully aware of how much his mother's unavailability has hurt him. He is enraged with her and probably has been for most of his life without realizing why. But the stress of her death led the way to an unconscious ambivalence about Frank's judgment of his mother, and more importantly, the mixed feelings that those judgments evoked. It is the not quite conscious (the pre-conscious) realization of his mother's inadequacies that kept Frank up at night.

Line 20. The counselor acknowledges Frank's anger as well as his courage in facing his previously unconscious "demons." She is aware that, since no mother is perfect, most (if not all) people harbor feelings of both love and hate for their mothers. The counselor might have lectured Frank about respecting his parents and loving them, but she knows that in the human condition, intense hatred is often the other side of the coin from genuine love.[8]

Line 21. Once Frank's unconscious belief that his mother was "a bitch" becomes conscious, the intense emotions associated with that belief are dissipated. The burden of his own anger has been lifted.

Line 22. The counselor knows that Frank's grief work is not

---

[8] This assertion will be explained in the following chapter.

yet finished. He will need to forgive his mother and recognize that he can love her in spite of her inadequacies. But Frank is so relieved that at this time he is not aware that there is work yet to do. So the counselor invites Frank to call her, when or if he recognizes that grief over the loss of his loved and hated mother is not fully resolved until he has forgiven her.

Biblical and Theological Reflections

There was nothing overtly Christian about the fictitious counseling session presented above. The counselor did not quote scripture or launch into a theological discourse on the commandment to honor our fathers and mothers. But Frank was relieved of a burden that was causing him great distress because the counselor accepted him, listened empathically to him and did not make judgments about him. This is the essence of Christian counseling even though the theory that informs the counselor, Psychodynamic Theory is not only secular but in many ways, anti-biblical.

Despite its lack of biblical or theological foundations, Psychodynamic Theory is very familiar to the Christian counselor because we also use the art of interpretation in our religious practices. That is, whenever we read scripture we are reading the words and looking to the Holy Spirit to help us to read between the lines, to interpret what we read.

For example, the words of the twenty-third psalm are a comfort and encouragement for everyone who reads them. But it is the meaning behind the words that provides us with such rich spiritual nourishment. "The Lord is my shepherd…" resounds in our souls because we interpret the word "shepherd" as one who watches over, protects and cares about his sheep. We choose to ignore the fact that the actual shepherd in the psalmist's time was likely to be a very rough character who might just as readily desert the flock as protect it. We interpret the printed words by associating the words with other words in that context. We associate "shepherd" with the following words of the psalm "I shall not want."

This is precisely what Christian counselors who use

Psychodynamic Theory do. They interpret the counselee's words within the context of that person's life in order to discover the deeper meanings of that individual's experiences. In fact, everyone who reads and interprets scripture in order to discover deeper meanings that are relevant to the reader is functioning like a psychoanalyst. And most would agree that their richest discoveries about the meaning of scripture are the result of the enlightenment of the Holy Spirit. This is also the experience of Christian counselors when they interpret the words and feelings of a counselee.

The practice of psychoanalysis does have the potential for opening the door to the work of the Holy Spirit. But the theory itself is in many ways reprehensible, especially to Christians. Sigmund Freud taught that we human beings are nothing more than intelligent animals driven by animal instincts (Freud, 1969). He wrote that Christianity is nothing more than an illusion for people who need to be psychoanalyzed (Freud, 1989). He tried to cast doubt on the teachings of the Pentateuch in his book *Moses and Monotheism* (Freud, 1967).But he also had something to offer to the art of Christian counseling. The specific concepts presented in this chapter are not Christian ideas, but neither are they antithetical to Christian teachings.

Questions to Consider

1) How does Freud's understanding of human nature (that we are simply cognitively evolved animals) compare with your own?

2) Can you recall an unconscious motive that later became conscious?

3) In what ways is your relationship with your spouse similar to the one between yourself and one of your parents?

4) As you read the dialogue between Frank and the counselor, were you able to "read between the lines" of his story. Compare your responses with those of the counselor.

5) What do you think about the concept of resistance? Should the counselor insist that the counselee sees "the truth" about himself or herself?

6) When you have counseled with people, do you often try to make them feel better by denying negative self-perceptions? What are the pros and cons of such an approach?

7) Did you find that the conversation between Frank and the counselor violates any scriptural or theological principles?

REFERENCES

Freud, S. (1967) K. Jones (trans.). *Moses and Monotheism.* New York: Vintage Books.

Freud, S. (1969) J. Strachey, (ed. & trans.). *An outline of psycho-analysis.* New York: Norton and Co.

Freud, S. (1989) J. Strachey (ed. & trans.). *The future of an illusion.* New York: Norton and Co.

Herman, J. (1992). *Trauma and recovery.* New York: Basic Books.

SUGGESTED READING

Brenner, C. (1982). Transference and counter transference. In *The mind in conflict* (pp. 194-212). New York: International Universities Press.

Cooper, A. (1989). Concepts of therapeutic effectiveness in psychoanalysis: A historical review. *Psychoanalytic Inquiry,* 9 (1), pp. 4-25.

Freud, S. (1901). *The psychopathology of everyday life: Standard edition, 6,* 1-310. London: Hogarth Press.

Greenson, R (1978). *Explorations in Psychoanalysis.* New York: International Universities Press.

Schafer, R. (1982). *The analytic attitude.* New York: BasicBooks.

Usher, S. (1993). *Introduction to psychodynamic psychotherapy techniques.* New York: International Universities Press.

CHAPTER II
From Sex To Relationships: Object Relations

The techniques described in the previous chapter are also used by Christian counselors whose ministries are informed by Object Relations Theory. This more recent theory shares with its theoretical forerunner the belief that better self-understanding leads the way to greater well-being in the life of the counselee. But counselors who are informed by Object Relations Theory differ significantly from psychoanalysts who accept Freud's understanding of human nature.

Sigmund Freud taught that personality development depends primarily on the gratification, or the lack thereof, of two motivations or instincts - sex and aggression. But Object Relations Theory is much more focused on the relationships of the counselee, both past and present, than a strict Freudian would be. While both theories are interested in the development of an individual's personality, Object Relations is based on the belief that individual personality is formed within the context of a relationship. Sex and aggression as motivating forces are much less important for object relations theorists.

Relationships are of paramount importance to the development of personality because it is in our interactions with others, especially during our formative years, that the core of the personality is created. Every human being eventually comes to recognize that he is a separate individual, that he is unique and therefore unlike any other person. Those who accept Object Relations Theory believe that the uniqueness of the individual is actually defined by his relationships with others.

The emphasis on relationships, however, may present a practical problem for counselors who use this theory. The counselor who is informed by Object Relations Theory may find that much of the counseling session focuses on people other than the counselee who should be the main concern in the therapeutic process. This could be highly problematic for the inexperienced counselor.

For many people, talking about a relationship means talking about the other person instead of the interaction of self and other. When this happens, the counselor might ask about how *the counselee* feels about the person he is talking about. The inclination to avoid talking about *both* self and other may require the counselor to repeatedly ask about the *self*-who-interacts with others when counselees are more comfortable talking about other people than they are talking about themselves.

Sometimes a counselee will talk about other people who have caused her nothing but pain. She describes a series of relationships that can only be described as self-defeating. For example, "Jenny," describes a relationship with a friend from early childhood who betrayed her by divulging a secret, then a husband who betrayed her by having an affair and then a business partner who betrayed her by stealing money from her. It is clear that there is a pattern of relationships in which the common theme has been betrayal. There is, however, another common factor in these relationships - Jenny, the counselee herself.

As a small child, Jenny felt betrayed by her mother whose love and attention were initially focused exclusively on her. Then, when her mother had a second child, that love and attention were withdrawn (from Jenny's perspective) and given to another. Because of this perceived betrayal, Jenny has an unconscious expectation that others would also betray her. And her expectations may have been self-fulfilling prophecies.

So the counselor invites Jenny to look at her own contributions to those relationships. Did her expectation of betrayal lead to a lack of good judgment about others? Was she attracted to people who were untrustworthy? Or, is her self-definition so entirely focused on being a victim that she needs to be betrayed in order to maintain a cohesive sense of who she is?[9] Addressing these issues will enable Jenny to gain a better understanding of who she is and how her beliefs about herself affect her interactions with others.

As this example suggests, it is during the formative years, from birth to around five years of age, that the child forms her own very subjective perceptions of her interactions with her mother. Objectively, Jenny's mother did not betray her daughter when she shifted her attention to a newborn. But Jenny interpreted her mother's changed interactions with her as a betrayal. This very subjective interpretation of the relationship with mother became a mental representation of that relationship. It is this mental representation that is the "object" in Object Relations Theory.

The subjectivity of the mental representation, the object, cannot be over stated. The infant/child does not make a clear distinction between what is subjectively experienced and what is objectively true. She only knows that her wants and needs are either satisfied or they are not. So part of every child's object is a "bad" mother, the mother who did not always give the child what she wanted when she wanted it. Fortunately, most children will also form a part-object that is a mental representation of a "good" mother. Again, the labels "bad" and "good" have little to do with the mother herself. They are the infant's and child's subjective experience of her.

As the child continues to interact with the "bad" mother, she will form a "bad" self. In Jenny's case, she felt betrayed by her mother when a younger sibling usurped her position as a much loved only child (a situation that has been referred to as the dethroned queen syndrome). As a result, Jenny was very angry with her mother. She began to vociferously demand attention, she even tried to hurt the usurper to her throne. The "bad" mother had given rise to the "bad" self.

If Jenny's mother had played with her again and given her

---

[9] These are not necessarily the questions that Jenny should be asked to answer. They are only indicative of the issues that she will eventually need to address.

special attention, then the child who interacted with the "good" mother would form a "good" self. Apparently, for Jenny the "good" mother was less present in her life so the "bad" mother became the more powerful influence in Jenny's mental representation of her. Just as importantly, Jenny's interactions with the "bad" mother were the more powerful influence in Jenny's mental representation of herself.

As this example indicates, over a period of several years, the object will come to include: (1) the good (need-gratifying) mother, (2) the bad mother who does not gratify the infant's/child's needs on demand, (3) the good self who interacts with the good maternal object and (4) the bad self who interacts with the bad maternal object. (Fairbairn, 1952). Eventually, the good mother and bad mother part-objects will be integrated, as will the good and bad self part-objects. But until then, any one or more of the part-objects may be separated from the rest of the object and repressed into the unconscious. These part-objects are split off because they would feel too threatening for the infant's and later the child's physical survival and/or emotional well-being.

For example, if part of the mental representation of the mother is one who consistently fails to gratify the needs of the infant/child, then that part is repressed and out of the conscious awareness of the child. Why? Because the child must believe that his mother loves and cares for him. Without her his very survival is threatened. Of course, the child will be frustrated and angry with the bad mother. So in addition to the bad mother being split off from conscious awareness, so too is the bad self. The reason for putting the bad self into the unconscious is that only the good self, the one who is loving and obedient will get at least minimal care from his mother.

The development of this complex, four-part object takes place over several years and goes through five stages. An understanding of each of the five stages of the development of the mental representation, the object, will help the counselor recognize the developmental stage that is currently causing a problem for a particular counselee.

The importance of recognizing how problems at a much earlier age affect a person's life in the present cannot be over stated. For example, when a counselee talks about a specific problem, the counselor can either address that problem directly or help the counselee understand the cause of that problem and many others like it. If the cause is out of the awareness of the counselee, then the counselor can be most effective by making the unconscious conscious. In order to do that, however, it is necessary to know what those unconscious elements might be. Knowledge of the five stages in the development of the object will go a long way in helping the counselor make conscious the unconscious elements.

The first stage in the development of the object is normal autism (not to be confused with the disorder known as Autism). This stage lasts from birth to about six weeks of age. For the newborn, the relationship with his mother is almost a continuation of his prenatal experience. He is aware of himself and in broad terms he is aware of his physical environment but he is not aware that his caregiver is a separate and distinct person. From the newborn's perspective, he and his mother are enmeshed, they are as one. It is not until later, when the infant begins to realize that his needs are not met immediately, that he achieves the realization that mother and he are actually two separate entities (Mahler, 1975). During this first stage, then, the object consists of one entity, mother/newborn.

By the time the child is about six months old, he is already expressing a need for some separation from those on whom his life depends. His former need for instant gratification partially gives way to a need to be an individual, separate and distinct from his mother. This is what is called the hatching stage (*ibid*). It is during this stage that the infant's sense of himself as a separate being increases so that now the object includes two entities, mother and infant.

Within a few short months, when the toddler is capable of walking and actually moving away from his caregiver he is expressing his individuality in no uncertain terms. That is, he is not only a *separate* person, he wants to be his *own* person. This third stage is the practicing stage, during which the toddler is rehearsing his capacity for mobility and in the process expressing his growing need for independence (*ibid*). He is also expressing his individuality verbally. Most children learn to say "no" very early, probably because they hear the word so often. But they use the word at every opportunity in order to insist that they are their own persons. The toddler has moved beyond a perception of himself as a body-self (hatching stage) and is beginning to experience himself as an emotional-social individual.

It is during this stage that the mental representations of both self and mother continue to develop and strengthen. What had been a two-part object (self and other) becomes a four-part object; the good mother, the bad mother, the good self and the bad self.

The fourth stage of development is the rapprochement stage (*ibid*). During this stage the child's curiosity brings him into the larger world. But the larger world can sometimes be frightening so he periodically returns to mother for comfort and reassurance. He wants to be an explorer but he also wants to know that he can come back to a safe place when he needs one. It is up to the parents to let the child explore his world (within safe limits) and also be available to him when he returns. This back and forth movement is sometimes difficult to manage for both children and parents. If there is significant pathology during this stage, one or more of the four part-objects will be repressed into the unconscious.

The final stage of development begins when the child is about four or five years old. This stage, called object constancy (*ibid*), is the period during which the child must recognize that the good mother (the one who meets his needs on demand) and the bad mother (the one who delays gratification of his needs) are one in the same person. The two perceptions of the mother must begin to be integrated as the child eventually relates to a whole person rather than to either a good mother or a bad mother. As the child integrates the mental representation of the good and bad mother, he integrates the good and bad selves that are also parts of the object.

A dysfunctional relationship during any of these five stages of development leads to dysfunctions later in life. For example, if the earliest stage is continued for a long period because the mother enjoys the exaggerated intimacy of enmeshment, then later in life the child, who is now an adult, will expect that everyone in his life will know and immediately meet his every need. That is, he repeats the initial relationship with his mother as he interacts with significant others in his life.

The hatching stage marks the beginning of a period of separation anxiety. The infant knows that he and his mother are separate and that knowledge is a two-edged sword. He is moving toward being an individual, an innate process present in every living being, but he is also aware that he could lose the one who sustains him. If the infant suffers a prolonged period of separation from his primary caregiver during this period, then later in life he may suffer intense grief and anxiety when he is threatened with even the temporary separation from a loved one.

During the practicing stage, a child who is not allowed an appropriate degree of independence (choosing his own toys, deciding which healthy foods to eat, etc.) may have a difficult time asserting his independence later in life. He may relate to others as if they, like his mother, will not respect his independent choices. He may also believe that he is not capable of making good choices because that was his subjective perception of his mother's attitude toward him.[10]

Failures during the rapprochement stage of development also lead to problems later in life. If mother does not allow her three year-old to explore his environment, then the child may be painfully fearful of new experiences. Or, if his mother was not available to him when he returned from his explorations, then he may be painfully dependent on others whom he needs to be emotionally available to him, a need exacerbated by a mother who was not there for him when his emotional development depended on it.

Perhaps the most common developmental failure occurs during the stage of object constancy. The result of dysfunction in this stage is to categorize self and/or others as either good or bad. It is difficult to maintain any kind of relationship if, when one discovers a flaw in a friend, the friend is perceived as no longer worth having. It is just as difficult to accept oneself as a flawed but acceptable human being if the good/bad self has not been integrated.

---

[10] After the hatching stage the use of the word "mother" is actually a shorthand expression for both parents.

The Christian counselor is well served when he or she has at least this rudimentary understanding of the development of the object, which is the core of one's personality. The dysfunctional relationships of early childhood are clearly recognizable later in life, as the following fictitious counseling sessions illustrate.

Fictitious Counseling Session I

Sam is a small, thin man in his mid-forties. He does odd jobs in his rural neighborhood. He is married and has no children. His wife works full-time as a music teacher. The counselor is the pastor of a church in the village in which Sam lives. They met in the pastor's church office.

Line 1. Sam: My wife and I are having real problems. We've been married for seven years but lately things are going badly. *(Long pause)*.

Line 2. Counselor: Can you be more specific about the problems?

Line 3. Sam: Well, when I get home from work I expect her to have the supper on the table. On the days that I work she gets home before me, and sometimes I have to wait while she's still fixing the meal. *(Pause)*. She knows I like cake but she still asks me what I want for dessert.

Line 4. Counselor: How does she know you like cake?

Line 5. Sam *(angrily)*: Well, after all this time she ought to know what I like for dessert!

Line 6. Counselor: You've never actually told her what you want?

Line 7. Sam: I shouldn't have to tell her, she should know.

Line 8. Counselor: You would like your wife to know what you want without telling her, to be like a Siamese twin joined to you at the head and at the heart. Instead she acts like she's an individual with her own head and heart.

Line 9. Sam: Well, when you put it that way. *(Long pause as Sam seems to withdraw emotionally)*.

Line 10. Counselor: I think I just hurt you.

Line 11. Sam: Well, yea, I guess you did. I guess the truth hurts. I need to think about what you said. *(Sam gets up to leave).* Well, thank you, pastor. What do I owe you?

Line 12. Counselor: Oh, no charge. But I am curious about something. Are you in a hurry?

Line 13. Sam: No, I can stay.

Line 14. Counselor: I'm just wondering why you decided to talk to a pastor about your marriage.

Line 15. Sam: Well, the price is right *(smiling)*. But really, that's not the only reason. You know, my mom used to bring me to this church every Sunday when I was a kid. But I haven't been to church for a long time.

Line 16. Counselor: What made you stop coming?

Line 17. Sam: Well, after my mother died, I was pretty lonely. I was very lonely. I kept asking God to give me a good woman who would love me but I didn't meet my wife until six years after my mom died. God didn't seem to care about whether I was hurting or not.

Line 18. Counselor: It seemed like God didn't care when He didn't answer your prayers?

Line 19. Sam *(crying):* Yeah, you can sure say that again.

Line 20. Counselor *(long pause):* I'm sorry to hear that, Sam. *(Sam gets up to leave).* I hope you know that you can stop by whenever I'm in the office. *(Smiling)* at least the price is right.

Line 21. Sam *(smiling):* Yeah, thanks.

Analysis

Line 1. From the very beginning, Sam seems to expect that the counselor should know what is troubling him. He also indicates that the problem is not with himself but with the marriage - an assumption made by most people with marital problems.

Line 2. The fact that Sam needs to be asked for specific information about his problem is a clue for the counselor. Sam apparently expects her to know what he's thinking and what he wants without actually telling her.

Line 3. As Sam explains the problem with his marriage it

becomes clear that he has little if any regard for his wife as a person who is separate and distinct from himself. He expects his needs to be met on his schedule and without his even voicing what those specific needs might be.

Line 4. The counselor invites Sam to question his assumption that his wife should know what he wants without him telling her. The counselor could have tried to make some concrete suggestions about how Sam might improve the relationship with his wife. For example, Sam might actually help her to prepare their meal, or tell her what he likes for dessert. But the counselor is knowledgeable about the stages of development that were described in this chapter. Her knowledge helps her avoid inconsequential interpretations and/or advice as she focuses on the developmental issues that have probably plagued all of Sam's relationships.

Line 5. Sam seems quite indignant. He does not recognize that his expectations of his wife, that she should be like the enmeshed maternal object, are unreasonable.

Line 6. The counselor questions Sam, inviting him to focus on his own contribution to his marital problems.

Line 7. But Sam seems either unwilling or unable to realize that he might contribute to his own unhappiness. He makes it clear that his wife is the problem. She is supposed to know what he wants without being told.

Line 8. After several invitations to Sam that he look at himself and his own inappropriate expectations, the counselor makes it clear to Sam what it is that he is not aware of. She makes the unconscious conscious.

Line 9. Sam shows real maturity as he accepts the counselor's interpretation especially because he (understandably) seems hurt by it.

Line 10. The counselor realizes that her interpretation was harsh, and she could feel Sam withdrawing emotionally so she gives him an opportunity to say that her comments were hurtful. She did not apologize for her harsh statement because to do so would have been perceived as taking away from the truthfulness of the interpretation. Perhaps even more importantly, an apology would have taken away the opportunity for Sam to express his anger about what the counselor said.

Line 11. Sam is honest about being hurt. But rather than allow the counselor an opportunity to address the hurt, he starts to leave. His offer to pay the counselor could be interpreted as an acknowledgment that she has been helpful. It seems more likely, however, that the offer to pay is meant to cancel any debt that he might owe the counselor. She provided a service and he will pay for it so that puts an end to the relationship.

Paying for a counseling session assures the counselee that he has no further obligations to the counselor. The counselee is not obligated to take the counselor's suggestions, to hide his anger or meet any other social requirements. By paying for counseling he has met his only obligation.

For the non-professional counselor, however, receiving payment is probably not appropriate because it implies that the counselor is professionally trained and certified. Instead of payment, the counselor could have allowed Sam to meet the obligation that he thought he had by suggesting that he make a contribution to the church or some organization of Sam's choosing.

Line 12. The counselor offers Sam a way to pay her that does not include money. He can do her the favor of satisfying her curiosity.Because she respectfully asked Sam (after they had attended to his agenda), her own agenda did not interfere with his.

Line 13. Sam may be curious about what the counselor has in mind so he agrees to stay.

Line 14. There are many subjects that counselee's choose not to talk about. Most people are uncomfortable talking about sex, money, politics and other issues, including religion. It takes a great deal of sensitivity for the Christian counselor to know whether or not to introduce religion and spirituality into the conversation with a particular counselee. The fact that Sam came to see the pastor in the church, however, provided some evidence that Sam might be amenable to talking about his relationship with God. This fact influences the counselor's decision to bring up Sam's religious experience.

Line 15. Apparently the counselor's intuition was correct. Sam was comfortable talking about his religious experience and what he said was very important. He associates his mother with going to church.

Line 16: The counselor could have guessed why Sam stopped coming to church. It probably had something to do with his mother. But she does not try to lead Sam in a particular direction, she asks a rather open-ended question.

Line 17. Sam's response is not surprising. He indicates that his spiritual development is at the same stage as his emotional development. Just as he expected that his wife should be like his enmeshed mother, Sam also expected that God would meet his needs "on demand."

Line 18. The counselor simply opens the door for Sam to reflect on what he has just said. She does not offer a biblical or theological defense of God or a sermon on the efficacy of prayer. Spiritual growth, like emotional growth often takes place in a safe and caring relationship. There is surely a place in ministry for sermons and biblical discourse, but this was not it.

Line 19. Obviously, the counselor touched a very painful place in Sam. After the earlier embarrassment (line 8) he now seems to have felt understood and accepted enough to be vulnerable in the counselor's presence. When the Christian counselor is faced with a choice between preaching and living the gospel, it is often the latter that is more beneficial to the counselee.

Line 20. The counselor chose not to pursue Sam's belief that God does not care about him. She believed that he had made himself vulnerable for a brief period of time and that was as much as Sam could handle. When he got up to leave, she ended their conversation with a joke ("the price is right"). This is seldom a good idea, but in this case it seems appropriate. Sam needed to go out and face the world, but to leave so soon after crying would have left him feeling even more vulnerable. The little bit of humor seems to have helped Sam move away from his obvious grief over the loss of his mother and his profound disappointment with a God whom Sam felt did not love him.

Line 21. Sam and the counselor began the session as strangers. For a brief period they were almost antagonists. But they part as two human beings who have encountered a profound experience together. Sam's demeanor and his "thank you" may be an indication that their relationship will continue in such a way as to begin to heal the wounds inflicted forty years before.

It is clear that during the normal autism stage of development, Sam's primary caregiver met her own need for the closeness (enmeshment) that mothers experience with their newborns. She may have felt closer to her baby than she ever has to anyone else in her life, and it felt good. The effect on Sam, however, was that he never matured to the point of recognizing that other people in his life were separate and distinct human beings with whom the relationship could be intimate while each maintained his or her own individuality.

If Sam is able to address the relationship with his wife by recognizing that she can love him without meeting his unspoken needs on demand, then he may also be able to relate to God in a more mature way as well. He can begin to understand that being loved and being taken care of as if he was an infant are two very different things.

Fictitious Counseling Session II

Bruce and Ann have been married for three years. They do not attend church but Bruce decided he needed to talk to someone so he went to see the pastor of a local congregation.

Line 1. Bruce *(anxious and hurried)*: I'm sorry to just drop in on you like this Father, but I have to talk to someone.

Line 2. Counselor: I'm glad you came.

Line 3. Bruce *(long pause)*: So, should I just tell you what's wrong?

Line 4. Counselor: Yes, please do.

Line 5. Bruce: I'm really desperate. My wife has left me.

Line 6. Counselor: Oh, I'm sorry to hear that.

Line 7. Bruce *(crying)*: She went to her mother's funeral yesterday. We've never been apart before. We've been married for three years and she's never been away overnight. I just don't know what to do. I can't sleep, I can't even go to work. I just don't know how I can manage without her. What should I do?

Line 8. Counselor: You're really upset.

Line 9. Bruce: Yeah *(deep breath)*.

Line 10. Counselor: Being apart from your wife is really painful for you. It feels like you've lost her?

Line 11. Bruce: Yeah, it feels that way. But you know, I haven't really lost her. She'll be back the day after tomorrow. But she better not do this to me again. Ever.

Line 12. Counselor: You're angry with her.

Line 13. Bruce: She's torn my life apart. You bet I'm angry with her.

Line 14. Counselor: And you're angry because…?

Line 15. Bruce: Because she left me *(long pause)*. Well, she really didn't leave me, she's coming back. I know that she had to go to her mother's funeral and we couldn't afford for me to go with her.

Line 16. Counselor: You seem to be saying that you let your emotions run away from you. Your fear is that she's left you for good, but you know that she'll be back.

Line 17. Bruce: Yeah, I did let my emotions get away from me. She calls me whenever she can, I know she loves me and now that I'm not so scared, I know she'll be back. Thanks, Father.

Analysis

Line 1. Bruce's demeanor is a good indication that he is very distraught.

Line 2. The counselor has never met Bruce and has no idea what his problem is, so he can do nothing for Bruce at this moment but be a good host.

Line 3. Talking to someone about his unhappiness is something very new for Bruce. He doesn't know what to do any more than does the counselor.

Line 4. The counselor doesn't want to lead Bruce into something that is not relevant for him, so he simply invites Bruce to continue.

Line 5. The reason for Bruce's desperation now becomes clear, or does it?

Line 6. Given what Bruce has just said, the counselor can only assume that Bruce's wife has left him permanently. But he can't be sure so he simply responds with an expression of sorrow.

Line 7. Now Bruce makes his situation clearer. Then he asks the counselor for advice. Many counselees will ask the counselor what they should do, but they are often asking for support rather than specific instructions.

Line 8. Recognizing that Bruce is much too upset to actually want to be told what to do, the counselor responds to Bruce's emotional state.

Line 9. The simple acknowledgement of Bruce's pain seems to have been a real blessing, as indicated by his deep breath - a sigh of relief.

Line 10. The counselor realizes that the current circumstance (Bruce's wife's temporary absence) is not the whole story. He assumes that her absence opens an old wound for Bruce, one that he is probably unaware of since it happened when he was an infant.

During the hatching stage, Bruce's mother was either physically or emotionally unavailable to him. Since as an infant, Bruce's very survival depended on his primary caregiver, her absence was terrifying for him. Now Bruce is re-living the terror of his infancy even though, as an adult, he is perfectly capable of taking care of himself.

Line 11. The counselor's understanding of Bruce's fears allows Bruce to be more realistic about his current relationship. His wife is not his mother. Her absence may feel life-threatening but Bruce can now look at the situation more rationally.

Line 12. It's important for Bruce to recognize his own anger at his wife/mother because his feelings could have a very bad affect on his marriage. His wife will probably be glad to be back and she will probably expect that Bruce would feel the same way. If he greets her with anger, she will not understand it and that could lead to a problem in their relationship (especially since she is just returning from her mother's funeral).

Line 13. Fortunately, Bruce recognizes that he is angry, although he doesn't understand the reason for his anger.

Line 14. In a very subtle way, the counselor invites Bruce to be more rational. He uses the word "because" as a way to turn from feelings to thoughts and implicitly encourages Bruce to think about why he is feeling the way he is.

Line 15. Bruce feels heard and known and accepted. Now he is able to think instead of letting his feelings control him.

Line 16. The counselor enlarges on what Bruce has just said. In doing so, he alludes to the experiences of infancy when he felt that his mother would never come back to take care of him. There is certainly no need for the counselor to ask about Bruce's early childhood experiences because they are all too evident in his life as an adult.

The counselor did not need to interpret Bruce's relationship with his wife as a transference (which it is). Instead, the counselor dealt with the current relationship, which resulted in Bruce being able to differentiate for himself his feelings relating to his mother from those he has for his wife.

Line 17. The lost has been found, the blind has been made to see. Bruce can now relate to his wife like an adult instead of like a six to eight month old baby.

Fictitious Counseling Session III

Elizabeth is a twenty-three year old woman who will soon graduate from a Christian college with a degree in education. The counselor is actually a history professor whose class Elizabeth had taken the previous year. They met quite by accident in the school cafeteria.

Line 1. Elizabeth: Boy, have I got a problem. I have three job offers and I don't know which one to take.

Line 2. Counselor: Well, what are the pros and cons of each one?

Line 3. Elizabeth: Oh, I don't even know. They're all good offers, I'm just so confused.

Line 4. Counselor: You don't sound too happy about all these offers.

Line 5. Elizabeth: I suppose I should be happy that at least I'd have a job. Some of my friends don't even have any offers yet. But it's just too much. I look at each offer and they all seem great. I just don't know what to do.

Line 6. Counselor: Sounds like making a decision is hard.

Line 7. Elizabeth: I don't think I've ever had to decide anything in my entire life. My mom went to this school - she's a teacher too. I've always just kind of followed along, whatever. Now I'm really scared. What if I choose the wrong job?

Line 8. Counselor: What would happen if you chose the wrong job?

Line 9. Elizabeth: I could really louse things up, I could get fired!

Line 10. Counselor: So?

Line 11. Elizabeth *(long pause.):* So, I'd take some time off, and then I could probably get another job, maybe not even a teaching job. I've always thought about being a nurse.

Line 12. Counselor: And at least you will have made an important decision for yourself. But I wonder if you've asked for God's guidance about what job to take.

Line 13. Elizabeth: You know, I've been so upset that I've hardly been able to pray at all. But I feel so much better now that I think it's about time I got back to where I belong. I need to ask for God's guidance about this.

Analysis

Line 1. Elizabeth is very clear about her problem. The fact that she has three offers for a position indicates that she has many strengths. She is probably intelligent and responsible but she is having trouble making her own decision.

Line 2. The counselor proposes a rational approach to Elizabeth's problem.

Line 3. Elizabeth states that she's not just undecided (rational) she's confused (emotional).

Line 4. Picking up on the counselee's cue, the counselor responds to Elizabeth's feelings (she doesn't "sound happy").

Line 5. Elizabeth goes from feelings to a moral judgement (she *should* be happy) and then a behavioral perspective - what to *do* about the jobs she's been offered.

Line 6. Elizabeth has given the counselor several topics to which he might have responded but he chooses to interpret the last statement simply because it was the last one. By choosing to respond to Elizabeth's last statement, the counselor is following the course that Elizabeth is setting.

Line 7. The counselor's apparent understanding of Elizabeth's problem leads her to reveal more about herself. She believes that she is incapable of making the right decision because she has never made important choices before.

Line 8. Continuing to follow the counselee's lead, the counselor responds to Elizabeth's last sentence. But he moves away from a strict adherence to psychoanalytically informed object relations counseling to a more cognitive approach (to be described in chapter V).

Line 9. Elizabeth reveals her fears that she is not capable of making a good decision and she believes the result of even trying to do so would be catastrophic.

Line 10. The counselor challenges Elizabeth's belief that the wrong decision would be a disaster by simply inviting her to consider the realistic consequences of her own decision. This too is a technique of cognitive therapy.

Line 11. Elizabeth realizes that what seemed like a catastrophe just a minute ago could actually present an opportunity to pursue a career that was her own choice rather than simply follow her mother's career path.

Line 12. The counselor interprets the developmental issue that has caused Elizabeth so much consternation. It was Elizabeth's inability to trust her own decisions, not the number of job offers that was the problem. The counselor read between the lines of what Elizabeth was saying and interpreted the cause of her problem instead of trying to solve it for her. Now that she seems less anxious, the counselor brings her spiritual life into the conversation.

Line 13. Elizabeth was so upset by the need to make her own decision that she could not pray. And she did not turn to God for guidance in the first place because her spiritual development is reflected in her emotional development.

Both spiritually and psychologically Elizabeth was responding to a dysfunctional relationship during the practicing stage. From the psychological perspective, Elizabeth wants to make her own choices but has too little experience to do so with confidence. From the spiritual perspective, now that she understands that she is no longer dominated by her parents' decisions, she can approach God with the same understanding.

Elizabeth can ask God for guidance without fear that God will overwhelm her growing autonomy. She can seek God's will for her life with the knowledge that obeying God's will is her own choice. God leads and guides but unlike Elizabeth's parents, does not coerce.

When she was a child, Elizabeth's parents may have made her decisions for her instead of letting her decide for herself. If Elizabeth wanted to climb the jungle gym or play with a safe pet, for example, she may have been told not to do so. Or her parents may have insisted on the clothes that Elizabeth wore or what foods she ate. If this was a consistent pattern through her early childhood, then she could have learned that it is only other people who are capable of making decisions and her own decisions were not to be trusted.

In object relations terms, Elizabeth developed a perception of her mother as the bad mother who restricted her growing need for independence. This bad mother part-object was eventually repressed into the unconscious so that Elizabeth didn't have to see herself as the rebellious (bad) child in relation to a restricting mother. But when it came time to exercise some independence, Elizabeth got scared. The unconscious bad mother evoked the fear that she could not trust her own decisions.

The question is, why now? Why did the unconscious part-object affect Elizabeth's capacity to choose what job to accept? The answer may be that Elizabeth became very anxious during a time of significant change in her life. She was about to leave the comparative safety of college in order to begin her life as a responsible adult. During any transitional stage, anxiety increases with the result that unconscious material (in this case, the bad mother part-object) exerts more influence over the person's life.

The Christian counselor did not ask Elizabeth about her early childhood experiences. He guessed that the current problem was probably caused by Elizabeth's perception of her relationship with her mother. Instead, the counselor focused on the problem at hand, which was Elizabeth's fear about making an independent decision. By doing so, the counselor opened the door to further emotional as well as spiritual development.

The counselor was wise not to make the mistake of telling Elizabeth what to do. What she needed was to exercise her own judgment. The counselor recognized this because he was knowledgeable about the stages of development of the mental representation of the mother-child relationship.

The counselor did not restrict himself to the techniques of Object Relations Theory but he did use its basic concepts. As a result, even though Elizabeth did not actually decide about a job she was able to consider options that were very different from her mother's choices for her. Her developing independence and autonomy will allow her to make this and future decisions more easily.

Perhaps the greatest gift that the counselor gave to Elizabeth was to remove the roadblocks to her seeking God's guidance. She seems to have related to God the way she did to her mother - that He too would make her do that which was not her own choice. Spiritual maturity is often delayed when there are developmental issues. Removing the threat of the bad mother part-object resulted in a greater trust in the loving guidance of a heavenly Parent who always respects our own free will.

Fictitious Counseling Session IV

Janet is in her mid-fifties and has recently separated from her husband after twenty-eight years of marriage. She and the counselor have been friends for many years. They attend the same church and go to the same Bible study class. The following conversation takes place after one of those classes.

Line 1. Counselor (to *Janet*): You were pretty quiet this

morning. Is every thing all right?

Line 2. Janet: Oh sure, I'm fine.

Line 3. Counselor: Good *(pause)*. Janet, You really don't seem fine.

Line 4. Janet: I guess I'm just a little tired *(long pause)*. You know what, actually I've been better.

Line 5. Counselor: Do you want to talk?

Line 6. Janet: Oh, I don't know *(long pause)*. Well, I don't want to bother you.

Line 7. Counselor: Janet, we've been good friends for how long? How many times have I poured out my problems to you?

Line 8. Janet: Yea, well…

Line 9. Counselor: Let's just sit here for a few minutes. No one's around, we can just be here for each other.

Line 10. Janet: Thanks *(weeping)*.

Line 11. Counselor: I guess life is tough for you right now.

Line 12. Janet: I've never been more miserable in my entire life. I am so horribly lonely, I'm so mixed up. I know I can't go back to my husband, but… I just don't know what to do.

Line 13. Counselor: We don't have to do anything. You know that I love you.

Line 14. Janet: *(Looks at her friend and quickly looks away as she hurriedly leaves the room)*.

Analysis

The two most revealing features of this counseling session are; first Janet's reluctance to admit that she is desperately unhappy and second her need to avoid talking about herself with her friend, the counselor. Even when the counselor reminds Janet that she has been a good friend to her Janet's response is minimal. When she eventually does give voice to her own suffering, Janet isn't telling the counselor anything that she couldn't see for herself, or anything that she couldn't have already guessed.

For her part, the counselor walks a fine line between being pushy and being supportive. The counselor realizes that Janet is feeling so fragile that the counselor must not be intrusive. Yet, she also realizes that Janet is in need of some emotional support. So the counselor offers nothing more than her presence, the presence of a friend. As is clear in line 10, this is exactly what Janet needs. She releases all of her intense feelings - she weeps. After Janet feels the relief that her crying provides, the counselor states the obvious, that "life is tough right now." That is enough for Janet to tell the counselor how she is feeling as well as her indecision about what she should do.

The counselor wisely refrains from offering a solution to Janet's problems. And then she responds from her *own* need to ameliorate her friend's pain by reminding Janet that she loves her. As Janet's response indicates, this was a mistake. The caring, understanding and empathic counselor felt a need to try to help Janet feel better and met that need by saying that she loved her. But in meeting her own need, the counselor offered exactly what Janet could not tolerate.

If Janet's behavior seems self-defeating, it's because it is. One would think that, given the suffering that Janet is clearly going through, she would welcome the counselor's support - her reminder that she loves Janet. But Janet not only didn't welcome it, she ran away from it. Why? The answer lies in Janet's relationship with her mother during the rapprochement stage of the development of the object.

When, as a toddler, Janet began to explore her world, her mother felt relieved that her daughter no longer demanded so much of her time and energy. So when Janet returned from her explorations looking for security and nurturing, her mother resented it. As a result of this oft-repeated interaction, the mental representation of her mother was that she is bad, she did not nurture when Janet needed it. And Janet's self-part of the mental representation was perceived as unworthy to be nurtured, she perceived herself to be the bad self in relation to the bad mother. The bad mother was then repressed into the unconscious because the feelings associated with her were just too painful. Unfortunately, the bad self continued to define Janet for the rest of her life.

Now that Janet is an adult she continues to feel unworthy of being supported or even consoled. The counselor understood that about Janet and did not try to do either - until line 13. The counselor gave in to her own need to nurture Janet and Janet basically ran away as a result of the counselor's momentary selfishness.

Janet rejects her friend's expression of love for two important reasons. First, it threatens her own self-perception, a crucial element of the mental representation that defines who she is. Now that Janet is feeling especially vulnerable, challenging her understanding of who she is seems intolerable to her. If she were to even question her self-perception, the core of her personhood, then the foundation upon which she interacts with her world could crumble - at least that is her fear. So she maintains a sense of cohesion and stability by maintaining a belief about herself (that she is unworthy of love and support) that can only add to her misery.

The second reason that Janet rejects her friend is that she so desperately *wants* to be nurtured and taken care of. But her need is so powerful that she is ashamed of it. She sees herself as needy, infantile and a loathsome burden to anyone who would want to help her. Janet feels only disgust with herself for needing other people so much. Her feeling of profound shame is greater than her need for a friend's care and love. So she runs away when she is offered exactly what she so desperately longs for.

Janet has conflicting needs, she needs to maintain a stable self-concept but she also has the human need to be loved and cared for by others. Her shame regarding her need to be loved only exacerbates the problem. In order to deal with this painful conflict, Janet may need professional help. Hopefully, when Janet is more stable, she and the counselor will resume their friendship and when the time is right the counselor can suggest that Janet might talk to a professional counselor.

Fictitious Counseling Session V

Richard is twenty-two years old, unmarried and living with his parents after flunking out of college. He is unemployed while he tries to decide what kind of job he wants to have. He came to talk to the counselor because he and his parents are fighting all the time.

Line 1. Richard: (*Slumps into a chair, pulls his cap over his face and says nothing for several minutes*).
Line 2. Counselor: I guess you don't want to be here.
Line 3. Richard: No I don't. My folks made me come.
Line 4. Counselor: They *made* you come?
Line 5. Richard: They said they'd throw me out of the house if I didn't.
Line 6. Counselor: What are they so mad about?
Line 7. Richard: They have all these rules; put my dishes in the dishwasher, put my dirty clothes in the laundry, don't play my music so loud. You know, all that parent stuff.
Line 8. Counselor: And you don't follow their rules?
Line 9. Richard (*angrily*): No, why should I?
Line 10. Counselor: I guess you don't like your parents any more than you do their rules.
Line 11. Richard: I hate them. They've never been there for me. Just because I flunked out of college they think I should get a job right away.
Line 12. Counselor: Wow, they must both be horrible people, real monsters. Sounds like they should both be in a mental institution at least. Or maybe put in prison for inhumane treatment of their own son.
Line 13. Richard: Well, they're not that bad.
Line 14. Counselor: Oh?
Line 15. Richard: I mean, they're okay. I am living in their house, I suppose I really should do some of my own chores, it wouldn't kill me.
Line 16. Counselor: They're not all bad. Anything good about them?
Line 17. Richard: My dad's okay. My mom has her moments too I guess.
Line 18. Counselor: Just like you, huh Richard?
Line 19. Richard: What does that mean?
Line 20. Counselor: I mean, they have their good points and their bad points, just like you.

Line 21. Richard: Yea, I guess you're right. Thanks.

Analysis

Line 1. Richard doesn't say a word, yet his behavior speaks volumes. He registers his lack of respect for the counselor by slumping in his chair, he pulls his hat over his face to let the counselor know that he is psychologically not present and refuses to speak.

Line 2. Given Richard's body language, the counselor can expect that her interpretation is quite accurate. The counselor could have chosen to interpret his behavior as rude or sullen or angry - but that would have been the counselor's own reaction. Instead she correctly chose to focus on Richard.

Line 3. Richard senses that the counselor is more interested in him than in her own feelings of being "disrespected" so he responds with real honesty. This indicates that he already has some degree of trust in the counselor.

Line 4. There were two possible issues for the counselor to address. One would be Richard's stated unwillingness to be there, the other is his relationship with his parents who apparently have a significant amount of influence over him. Either issue would be worth pursuing but addressing Richard's feelings about talking to a counselor is not his agenda.[11] Also, the counselor assumes that this will be the only counseling session with Richard (a good assumption to make with most counselees) so she chose the topic that is the problem of the present moment.

Line 5. It is unclear if Richard actually believes that his parents would throw him out of the house if he didn't come for counseling. It could be that their threat was just the extra motivation that Richard needed. His willingness to engage the counselor (after the initial reluctance to do so) may indicate that he is not there for his parents' sake alone but for his own sake as well.

Line 6. Richard did not say that his parents were mad at him,

---

[11] The therapeutic relationship is important. Without at least a measure of human connection nothing of value can take place in the counseling session.

although they probably are. The question suggests that the counselor may have identified with the angry parents.[12] The counselor should have monitored herself more closely and not fallen into a parental role herself. It would have been better to ask Richard about how he feels about his parents' threats.

A different counselor might have identified with Richard, especially if she lives with her parents and finds that experience to be difficult. When a counselor and counselee share similar life situations there is a danger that the counselor will not maintain appropriate objectivity.

Line 7. Richard reveals himself as he complains about his parents. He seems selfish, self-absorbed and irresponsible. The fact that he is living with his parents may be one reason for his immaturity. When adult children live with their parents the whole family may adopt previous patterns of behavior - in this case an adolescent pattern.

Line 8. Richard wants to talk about his parents and the counselor (appropriately) wants to talk about Richard. But the counselor asked the wrong question. She might have asked Richard how he feels about "all that parent stuff" or more specifically if he is angry with his parents about all their rules. Instead the counselor asks a question that is more accusatory than interpretive. Again, a failure on the counselor's part to acknowledge her own feelings about Richard's behavior has led her to being more parental than objective.

Line 9. Richard hears the counselor's criticism and expresses anger in a way that may be similar to the way he speaks to his parents, that is, transference has taken place. He treats the counselor the same way he treats his parents, in part because he needs to resolve the issue so he replicates it in the counseling session and in part because the counselor sounds like his parents.

Line 10. Richard's anger saves the counseling session. The counselor realizes that she was treating him the same way his parents do so she regains her own objectivity. She interprets his anger at them (and her) in such a way that he can accept it. She

---

[12] When the counselor assumes the role of the transferential figure (Richard's parents), this is called counter-transference - something that should be avoided.

suggests that he "doesn't *like* his parents" any more than their rules. This mild characterization could have been merely accepted or enlarged upon. It is difficult for many people to say that they hate their parents so "don't like" feels safer to them.

Line 11. Richard is angry enough to express his hatred, which is not only towards his parents but also possibly toward himself. He may see himself as a failure for flunking out of college even while he continues to blame his parents for his own unhappiness.

Line 12. The counselor interprets Richard's feelings by exaggerating how terrible his parents are. This is an unorthodox approach in object relations therapy but strict orthodoxy requires that each counselee be treated the same way. Since each person is unique, failure to follow the rules of any particular type of therapy can be a benefit to the counselee.

Line 13. The counselor's obvious exaggeration gives Richard an opportunity to reflect on what he has said and how he feels. In a more rational moment he begins to realize that his feelings may not be based on reality.

Line 14. The counselor does not want to get in the way of Richard's self-reflection and new understanding of himself and his parents. She simply asks an open-ended question as an encouragement for him to continue what he had already started in line 13.

Line 15. Richard reflects on who his parents are as human beings rather than on his mental representation of them. He begins to see them as actual individuals rather than the objects who exist in order to meet his needs and ease his own feelings of failure.

Line 16. Richard's capacity for a more objective perception of his parents was revealed rather suddenly. The counselor takes a chance that his previously bitter attitude toward his parents is rather recent and therefore more open to change. So she guesses that he is actually quite stable and speaks of the loved parents as just as real as the hated ones.

Line 17. Richard affirms the counselor's perception. He reluctantly agrees that his parents are not all bad.

Line 18. Now the counselor uses Richard's insights about his parents in order that he might gain some additional insights about himself.

Line 19. Richard is confused. The counselor's previous question has turned his attention from his parents to himself and he needs some time to change directions. His question indicates that he is mildly annoyed about this sudden change of focus but also curious enough to ask the counselor to clarify her remarks.

Line 20. The counselor is pleased to have this opportunity to summarize Richard's own insights regarding his parents and add some about Richard himself. (It is seldom that a counseling session includes such a neat wrap-up).

Line 21. Richard's attitude toward the counselor has changed. He gained some important insights about his feelings about his parents and more importantly, about himself. Like his parents, Richard is not all bad just because he failed in college.

Two points need to be made about this counseling session. First, it is fictitious. The resolution of problems is seldom as quick and easy as this case might suggest. The second point has to do with the "paradoxical intervention" by the counselor (line 12). That is, when Richard says he hates his parents, the counselor grossly exaggerates his statement. She does this in order to draw the counselee's attention to what he has just said. This catches Richard's attention and he re-thinks his own statement that he hates his parents.

To put it in biblical terms, the counselor used the same technique that Jesus used in many of his parables. Jesus turned the world upside down for those who heard Him and in doing so He taught them something that was hard for them to grasp. The paradoxical intervention accomplishes the same thing.

In this counseling session, the counselor avoids the temptation to focus on Richard's stated problem - that his parents make unreasonable demands on him. (If the counselor is the parent of adult children, then avoiding that temptation was a major accomplishment). Instead, the counselor focused on the relational problem - that Richard hates his parents. It wasn't until the counselor exaggerated Richard's feelings about his parents that he was able to integrate the split good and bad maternal (which includes his father) part-objects. Once these two part-objects were integrated, Richard could also integrate his good and bad self part-objects as well. During this brief counseling session, Richard was able to continue the task of the object constancy stage. He saw his parents and himself as neither good nor bad. Richard saw himself and his parents as human beings.

Biblical and Theological Reflections

Is Object Relations Theory suitable for use by the Christian counselor? Its emphasis on the development of self in relation to others is certainly an improvement over the earlier theory from which it was derived. But is there anything specifically Christian about this theory? Let me answer this question by telling you a story.

Once upon a time there was a man who lived with his father and mother. The three of them were of one mind about everything. They ruled over a kingdom in which all of the inhabitants lived in everlasting joy and peace and love. Then one day, the father sent his son to a place in which people were unhappy, they were filled with hatred and were unjust in their treatment of strangers in their land. In order to improve the lives of the people who lived in this unfortunate kingdom, the son made some very important decisions about where to go and who should join him in his efforts to teach people how to live richer and more fulfilling lives. But even while he made these decisions he would often go back to his father for comfort and solace as well as for advise about how to complete his mission. Then one day, some people who were threatened by his teachings and his very presence tried to kill him. But their efforts were thwarted because the son returned to his father and mother where they continue to rule as one to this day and forever.

This of course, is an allegory. The story could be about the development of a mental representation of the relationship of the parents and the infant/child. In the beginning, the parents and their son were one, as in the stage of normal autism. Then the son left his parents (the hatching stage). In the process of fulfilling his mission, the son began to form an independent self (practicing stage). Once he left his father and mother, the son found that his task was often disheartening so he returned often to his parents (rapprochement stage) before returning to his work. But eventually the son returned to his father's realm. The son, his mother and his father remained three separate persons but formed an integrated whole (the stage of object constancy) as they ruled their kingdom together.

With some creative imagination, the allegory could also be understood as a story about the life, death and resurrection of Jesus Christ. Is it just a coincidence that the stages of development of the object and the central story of the New Testament parallel each other? What does it mean that the two stories have so much in common? Of course, it does take a leap of imagination to see the commonalities, but such a leap could provide the Christian counselor with some valuable insights concerning the connection between the spiritual and the psychological problems of a counselee.

Once that leap of imagination has been taken, it is possible to see that a person's spirituality is just as much a part of his/her personality as other thoughts, feelings, motivations, behaviors, hopes, dreams, etc. If our imaginations allow us to make the leap, we might discover that just as the infant/child develops psychologically as he relates to his mother, there is a parallel spiritual development as we relate to God. If this is true, then the Christian counselor is able to address the inter-relatedness of the psychological and spiritual issues of his/her counselees.

This suggestion is illustrated by two of the fictitious counseling sessions that were presented earlier. In the fictitious case of Sam, for example, his spiritual journey was as delayed as was his psychological development - he was functioning as if he was still in the stage of normal autism. Apparently, Sam's understanding of God is that He, like Sam's wife, should gratify Sam's needs on demand. Of course, Sam's understanding of God could only lead him to disappointment. It is almost inevitable that Sam would simply give up on a God who "failed" him.

In the case of Elizabeth (practicing stage), she hesitated to seek the guidance of a heavenly Father who might coerce her into making a decision, which was how she perceived her parents.

Bruce's devastation resulted, on the surface, from his wife's temporary absence. But his feelings came more from a mother who did not adequately care for him when he was just beginning to realize that he and his mother were two different people (hatching stage). If he could not trust his wife to return to him after a brief trip, could Bruce ever trust God to be there for him? Is that the reason that he does not attend worship services?

Janet has issues stemming from the stage of rapprochement. She may spend her entire life avoiding the God who loves her (the way she did her friend) even while she continues to study God's word in hopes of being able to embrace His love. Another person with problems related to the same stage of development might forget all about God when life is good and return to Him when life got tough, just like a toddler would return to his mother when his adventures became too uncomfortable.

A person like Richard, who had not fully integrated the good/bad self and maternal part-objects during the stage of object constancy would probably reject God. This person would blame God for life's tragedies while he failed to acknowledge God's blessings in his life. Or, a person might love God and refuse to acknowledge the fullness of God who is both a loving Father and a righteous Judge.

In addition to being able to address a person's spiritual development as an integral part of his/her personality (when the counselee permits it), the Christian counselor who uses Object Relations Theory has the tools to give a gift from God to the counselee. In the fictitious counseling sessions presented earlier, the counselors listened, let the counselees know that they were truly known and yet they were not criticized or judged. To be known and accepted despite all of our faults is the essence of God's love for us. To give this same gift to another is nothing less than living the gospel.

The Christian counselor who gives the gift of love has initiated a process. It is impossible to know if that gift will stagnate and die in the life of the counselee or continue to express itself for years to come. Assuming that the counselor is a person of prayer, then there is every reason to believe that the prayers of the counselor, long after the counseling sessions have ended, will continue to water the garden in which the seeds were planted.

Questions to Consider

1) What is the difference between an object and a person?

2) Do you think the object or the actual person is the more powerful influence on the child's personality development? Why?

3) Do you know someone who exhibits characteristics of the first stage of development, the normal autism stage? What traits does this person have that lead you to your assessment?

4) Do you know someone who exhibits characteristics of the practicing stage? What traits does this person have that lead you to your assessment?

5) Do you know someone who exhibits characteristics of the final stage of development, the object constancy stage? What traits does this person have that lead you to your assessment?

6) How could you do more harm than good in working with Elizabeth? If she came back for a few more sessions, what would you focus on?

7) Do you believe that the counseling sessions presented in this chapter deserve the description of Christian counseling? Explain.

8) What is your reaction to the allegory comparing Object Relations Theory with the life, death and resurrection of Jesus Christ?

REFERENCES

Fairbairn, W. (1952). *An object relations theory of the personality.* New York: Basic Books.

Mahler, M, Pine F. and Bergman, A. (1975). *The psychological birth of the human infant.* New York: Basic Books.

SUGGESTED READING

Jacobson, E. (1964). *The self and the object world.* New York: International Universities Press.

Kohut, H. (1971). *The analysis of the self.* New York: International Universities Press.

Mahler, M, Pine F. and Bergman, A. (1975). *The psychological birth of the human infant.* New York: Basic Books.

Mitchel, S. (1988). *Relational concepts in psychoanalysis.* Cambridge: Harvard University Press.

Phillipson, H. (1955). *The object relations technique.* London: Tavistock.

CHAPTER III
Person-Centered Therapy

Carl Rogers, the founder of person-centered therapy, is arguably the most influential psychologist since Sigmund Freud. Rogers' beliefs about human personality were a reaction to the assumptions of the psychodynamic theories and their focus on the first few years of life as the period during which personality is formed.He believed that our personalities are created every day of our lives for our entire lives. For Rogers, personality is an on-going process, and most importantly, one that could be under the conscious control of the individual.

Another important distinction between the psychoanalytically informed therapies[13] and person-centered therapy is the role of the counselor. Rogers suggests that those who follow the Freudian model relate to the patient as any doctor would. The doctor/therapist is the expert who knows what the patient needs in order to help her feel better. The patient in turn passively accepts whatever the doctor has to say. This of course is an exaggeration of the doctor-patient relationship but it does have some validity for many such relationships.

The therapist who uses Rogers' person-centered therapy relates to the counselee in a very different way. The person-centered counselor assumes that each human being is his/her own best

---

[13] These therapies include psychoanalysis, object relations, self psychology and ego psychology to name a few.

therapist. The counselor's role is to provide a safe place, one in which the counselee feels accepted and affirmed, so that the counselee is able to pursue his/her own natural inclination towards well-being.

In order to provide a safe place for the counselee, the counselor must be a caring, accepting and empathic listener. For Rogers; knowledge of human development, understanding of psychological theories and the techniques that come from those theories is almost inconsequential. The most important element in counseling has to do with the person of the therapist. If the therapist is authentic, that is, if he knows and acts on what he truly feels and thinks, then the counselee will be able to be in touch with her own genuine self as she relates to a counselor who is genuine and compassionate (Rogers, 1995).

The assumption that it is the person of the counselor that is so important in the therapeutic endeavor is central to Rogers' theory and most counselors would agree with his assumption. Some of the other foundational beliefs of person-centered therapy, however, are not as widely accepted. These more controversial concepts have to do with innate human motivations. Specifically, Rogers believes that we are inherently driven towards increasing individualization. Related to individualization is the belief that human beings have an innate drive toward self-actualization. Each of these concepts requires some explanation.

By individualization, Rogers means the ability to develop our own unique personhood and in the process become separate from others while at the same time remain connected to them.[14] Perhaps the best description of individualization comes from the theologian Paul Tillich who wrote "The more individualized a being is the more [he] is able to participate. Man as the completely individualized being participates in the world in its totality through perception, imagination and action." (Tillich, 1957, p. 65). That is, each individual is separate and distinct from, but also participates in, the world in which she lives. To be an individual, then, means that a person is self-governing (autonomous) yet is able to interact

---

[14] Object Relations Theory suggests that this begins during the hatching stage and is more or less complete in five or six years.

with others without losing her own values and priorities (Rogers, 1995). These values and priorities can always be influenced by others, however, as the individual engages the world.

Every human being not only has an innate need for individualization, he/she also has an innate drive toward self-actualization (*ibid*). By self-actualizing, Rogers means a process of becoming who we choose to be. We are not predetermined by human nature or early childhood experiences to be who we are. Rather, we each have the potential to grow into the kind of person we decide to be now and in the future.

The crucial elements in the on-going process of self-actualization are awareness and choice (*ibid*). By awareness Rogers means self-awareness. This is not just a rational and objective concept of oneself, it is primarily a subjective experience.

The person who is self-aware recognizes his feelings, a kind of visceral awareness that then leads to a better understanding of the self who feels in the present and lives in the now. For example, a woman may insist that she loves her daughter. Her self-concept is that she has always been a good and loving mother. But as she experiences her own feelings of resentment, frustration, and anger with her daughter she must change the sense of who she is according to her current feelings. She realizes that she sometimes feels emotions that are not loving toward her daughter - she is not the mother she thought she was. Her self-awareness increases and becomes more complex as she experiences her emotions of the moment.

Choice is another important part of the self-actualizing process. Rogers places a great deal of emphasis on free will, on the human capacity to choose. For him we are, at any given moment, free to decide to be either genuine or phony. We can decide to be either an individual or a person who simply follows the crowd. We are not mere automatons who must engage in mob behavior and agree with the opinions and attitudes of others, we each have the free will to decide who we are despite the pressures of others who may disapprove of our choices.

The impulse to be self-actualizing is so strong that even children who grow up without the acceptance and affirmation of parents and community have a self-righting tendency (Masten, Best and Garmazy, 1990). Researchers have studied children from the most dysfunctional families and circumstances. They found that at least some of those children had amazing resiliency. They were engaged in the process of self-actualization.

The researchers interpreted their results by suggesting that there is something inherent in every human being that drives the individual toward achieving his/her own potential. That despite the circumstances under which individuals were raised, they find creative ways to make themselves good people who live good lives. They find a way to be self-actualizing.

Related to self-actualization is the idea of congruence. A self who is actualizing his own potential, one who is centered and whole is said to be congruent (Gurman and Messer, 1995). Perhaps the best way to explain congruence is to illustrate what it is not. If, for example, a child believes that her feelings and attitudes are unacceptable to her parents, she may decide to gain their approval by becoming who they want her to be.[15] It is as if she becomes like a tree that grows from two different roots. One part of the tree bears delicious fruit (the genuine self) and the other part bears fruit that looks delicious but is actually poisonous (the self who seeks to please others). It looks like one tree but lacks the integration that is required for a single tree to grow - it lacks congruence.

In order to achieve congruence, the person must acknowledge all of the various influences on his/her life and decide which ones will continue to affect him/her and which ones will not. The congruent self will bring together all of the disparate elements of who he/she is so that all of the voices in his or her head speak the same language.

Related to congruence is the concept of authenticity. When a human being is able to integrate his/her experiences into a relatively stable whole, then he/she can also be authentic. Such a person doesn't follow conflicting impulses because internal conflicts have been resolved. To be sure, the authentic person may be grumpy at times and happy at other times. She is sometimes playful and sometimes serious. But she is always genuine. The

---

[15] Object relations theorists call this the false self.

authentic person has been described as being "comfortable in his/her own skin." That is, he or she is real.

Carl Rogers places a high value on authenticity, which is a genuine expression of each individual's uniqueness. And that uniqueness is enhanced when we create our own sense of who we are (Rogers, 1995). As we live our lives we continually find new ways to adjust to other people and to the situations in which we might find ourselves. With each experience we re-create ourselves even as we experience ourselves as relatively stable and congruent.

These assumptions about what it is to be human inform the core of person-centered therapy. Since we have innate drives toward individualization and self-actualization, all that is required of the therapist is to allow the counselee to experience herself, especially her emotions, so that she might choose who she wants to be and creatively adjust to her new insights as well as the always-new challenges of her life. The counselor allows this normal unfolding of the healthy personality by giving his unconditional positive regard. This is actually an attitude rather than something that the counselor says or does. It is an attitude of empathic understanding without making judgments (either positive or negative) about the counselee.

One way to convey the counselor's attitude of unconditional positive regard is through reflective listening. As the name of the technique suggests, this means that the counselor reflects back to the counselee what she is feeling and what she seems to be thinking. The counselor interprets what the counselee is feeling by naming the emotion that he is experiencing with her. He interprets what the counselee may be thinking by using her own words. While the counselee's thoughts are important, it is her emotions that will usually be the focus of attention in this type of therapy.[16]

This emotional connection of the counselor to the counselee is the essence of the therapeutic relationship. It is the very heart and soul of person-centered therapy. Without it, nothing of value can happen but with it the counselee experiences herself more

---

[16] This of course, is not unlike the techniques of the psychoanalytically informed therapies even though the assumptions of person-centered therapy are so very different from the earlier ones.

profoundly. She creates herself anew, she chooses to be who she is rather than who others want her to be. She continues in her journey toward self-actualization.

The following fictitious counseling session will illustrate these concepts of person-centered therapy (also called Rogerian therapy) and the techniques that are derived from them.

Fictitious Counseling Session

Sally is a widow in her mid-forties who lives alone. She is the author of several books about spirituality. She attends the same church as the counselor.

Line 1. Sally: Hi, how are you?

Line 2. Counselor: I'm a little tired today, how are you?

Line 3. Sally: Well, I just spent over $1500 on car repair, my son called to let me know that he lost his job, my sister practically hung up on me the other day and my best friend is going into the hospital for major surgery.

Line 4. Counselor: You feel overwhelmed?

Line 5. Sally: Yes, I am overwhelmed. I haven't been sleeping well, I'm tired all the time, I don't know…

Line 6. Counselor: Overwhelmed and pretty down in the dumps?

Line 7. Sally: Yea, I guess I am (*long pause*). (*Crying*) I don't know what's wrong with me. This is not like me to get so upset over nothing. What's wrong with me?

Line 8. Counselor: You tell me.

Line 9. Sally: I guess I've just had a really bad week and it's getting to me. What I need is to take some time out. I need to go to bed and have a good cry. I need to get back to writing in my journal and I need some plain old-fashioned quiet time with the Lord. That's what I need!

Line 10. Counselor: You feel less discouraged?

Line 11. Sally: Yea, I do feel better. And you know what? I need to be more intentional about talking care of myself.

Line 12. Counselor: You sound pretty determined.

Line 13. Sally: I hate it when I sound like a sniveling idiot. I'm perfectly capable of solving my own problems. I don't need to come in here and complain about my life. Actually, my life is pretty good. I think if I made a habit of thanking God for all His blessings I'd probably be a lot better off.

Line 14. Counselor: You're angry with yourself?

Line 15. Sally: No, not angry really. Just disgusted that I think that I need to talk to someone in order to fix me.

Line 16. Counselor: You're disgusted with yourself?

Line 17. Sally: Maybe not disgusted, maybe... oh, I don't know.

Line 18. Counselor: Confused?

Line 19. Sally: I need to go home and take care of myself.

Line 20. Counselor: You feel uncomfortable when you need other people?

Line 21. Sally: What makes you say that?

Line 22. Counselor: Well, I'm feeling your discomfort.

Line 23. Sally: Well, I just meant... (*pause*) yea, I guess I am. it's true, I'm not comfortable asking other people for help. It makes me feel vulnerable. I don't like that feeling.

Line 24. Counselor: Vulnerable?

Line 25. Sally: Yea, you know. I could ask for help and then someone thinks I need them, I don't like that.

Line 26. Counselor: You don't like that?

Line 27. Sally: No, of course not. You ask someone to help you and they think they're God or something. They think that they can treat you like dirt and just because you asked for help that they can get away with it.

Line 28. Counselor: Is that the way you feel about me?

Line 29. Sally: Oh no. I didn't mean you. I meant other people. I trust you not to hurt me, but other people, you know how people can be. Mean. You can't trust them.

Line 30. Counselor: So in the past people whom you've asked to help you have treated you badly, but right now you don't feel like you're being treated badly.

Line 31. Sally: I trust you and I want to trust others, but I can't. My life is too full of people that I've trusted who have really let me down. But it does feel good to trust someone, to trust you. I'd

[75]

like to trust people.

Line 32. Counselor: You'd like to trust, but when people hurt you it really hurts - a lot.

Line 33. Sally: I guess if I were as independent as I think I am it wouldn't hurt me so much.

Line 34. Counselor: So, you're not as independent as you thought you were?

Line 35. Sally (*laughing*): I guess I'm not, not really. *(Pause)*. Maybe that's why I feel so anxious when I pray. I know that I love God, and I want to really believe that God loves me. But maybe I'm afraid to *need* God's love. Boy, that's ridiculous isn't it. What's wrong with needing God to love me?

Analysis

Line 2. The counselor actually answers Sally's question about his well-being. This in itself is a clear difference from a psychoanalytic approach and gives a good example of the authenticity of the counselor. He says that he is a little tired, indicating that Sally's question is taken seriously and that he does not feel the need to pretend that he is anything other than human - he gets tired. However, and just as importantly, the counselor quickly turns the conversation back to Sally without elaborating on his own condition.

Line 3. Sally unloads her burdens on the counselor whom she trusts will simply share them with her.

Line 4. The empathic response, "you feel overwhelmed" comes from Sally's list of problems and from the counselor's ability to feel what Sally is feeling and put it into words.

Line 5. Encouraged by the counselor's empathic response, Sally talks about her own feelings rather than the cause of those feelings. This brings the conversation "into the now" as opposed to the events of the last week or so.

Line 6. The counselor does not make a psychological diagnosis, he doesn't say that Sally is depressed. Rather, he speaks in everyday language. The counselor's response touches Sally in a very human and affirming way. She feels known and accepted and is able to trust the counselor with the depth of her emotions.

Line 7. When Sally asks the counselor "what is wrong with me"? she is implying two things. First, that the counselor is better able to determine what is bothering her than she is herself. Second, that there is something wrong with her - as if feeling sad and crying constitute a bad feeling and inappropriate behavior.

Line 8. Rather than interpret Sally's unspoken statements about not being the expert regarding herself and being wrong about her feelings and behavior, the counselor deflects the question. In person-centered therapy, the counselee is encouraged to discover for herself what is troubling her. It is self-discovery that is at the heart of this kind of counseling, not interpretations by the counselor.

The counselor does not respond to the question of the "wrongness" of Sally's feeling sad and crying. Sally has made a judgement about herself. The counselor may not feel comfortable about her self-criticism, but her feelings are the focus of attention, not his.

Line 9. Sally also ignores her own self-judgment and discovers for herself what she needs to do to take care of herself after a series of upsetting events.

Line 10. It may have been tempting for the counselor to approve of Sally's determination to take care of herself. The Christian counselor may have been even more tempted to approve of her attention to her own spiritual life. Both would have been judgments - positive judgments to be sure, but judgments nevertheless. The key to unconditional positive regard is that the counselor makes neither positive nor negative judgments, he accepts Sally for who she is without affirming (or criticizing) what she does. The counselor responds instead by reflecting back to Sally how she feels.

Line 11. Sally affirms her own decisions, possibly because the counselor did not. This is the essence of individualization. One's own feelings, thoughts and behaviors define oneself, not the opinions of others.

Line 12. The counselor reflects Sally's feelings back to her.

Line 13. Could it be that Sally is too independent? She refers to her crying as behaving "like a sniveling idiot." She condemns herself for needing the counselor. It is easy to confuse independence with simply not trusting others.

The person who has a healthy independence is capable of mutual interdependence. But Sally is critical of herself for being a human being who needs other human beings.

Line 14. The counselor does not respond to the issue of independence and interdependence, he again responds to Sally's emotion - this time of anger. Sometimes determination can sound like anger, but the counselor attended to Sally's determination *and* her emotional state, which he experienced with her.

Line 15. Sally is not in touch with her own feelings, or does not want to say that she is angry with herself. She seems to have a perception of what kind of person she wants to be, and it does not include needing others or being angry with herself. Self-perception is a powerful force in guiding one's behaviors, thoughts and relationships. As such, it is not easily changed. Sally denies being angry, she prefers to be "disgusted," which of course is a specific category of anger. She re-asserts her need to be independent.

Line 16. The counselor does not interpret this need, he doesn't even ask a question about Sally's exaggerated need for independence. Instead he repeats Sally's own word "disgusted."

Line 17. Sally has a difficult time seeing herself as experiencing any emotion related to anger, even when it's anger directed at herself. Now she's in a quandary. She had just said that she was disgusted with herself but now she wants to deny that feeling.

Line 18. The counselor suggests the word that Sally seems to be looking for - that she is confused. This is such a common temptation, but one that should be avoided. Instead of giving Sally enough time to name her own feelings, the counselor intruded on her thought process and said the word for her. In his desire to be helpful, he was not helpful as Sally's response clearly indicates.

Line 19. Sally needs to get away, to escape from the empathic counselor who now feels intrusive because of his unwanted "helpfulness." She repeats her earlier need to take care of herself and not need anyone else.

Sally also indicates that she can deal with the confusion about her own feelings. Actually, this is a very positive sign. A person's capacity to tolerate confusion and ambiguity is a good sign that he or she will continue to grow and develop into a self-actualized human being.

Line 20. Now the counselor moves away from merely reflecting back to Sally how she is feeling. His interpretation, as a departure from the previous method of reflection, seems to have startled Sally.

Line 21. Sally is surprised by the counselor's interpretation. She did not realize that her desire to go home and take care of herself implied a need for independence.

Line 22. The interpretation is certainly not one in which the unconscious material is made conscious, it more or less repeats Sally's comments back to her.

Line 23. Sally seems upset, unsure of what she wants to say. But she feels comfortable with the counselor and is not afraid to contemplate her own words, even when they indicate something about her that would make her vulnerable in a different setting.

Line 24. A simple but effective reflection back to Sally the word that she had used.

Line 25. The counselor's unconditional positive regard, his empathy and his simple reflections provide a safe place for Sally to reflect on her own feelings.

Line 26. Again, a simple reflection of Sally's feelings.

Line 27. It feels like Sally is angry - but she is more likely anxious and her anxiety is expressed as anger (a very common experience). It could be that she was anxious about what she is just about to say. She may not want to know about herself that she resents the way she has been treated by people to whom she has gone for help.

Line 28. The counselor asks if Sally feels that way about him. He could have responded more directly to Sally's feelings of either fear or anger. Instead, he focused on the all-important therapeutic relationship and allows Sally to be more aware of the here and now. The authentic self only exists in the present because it includes emotions that are felt at the time. So the counselor decides to focus on now.

Line 29. Sally's response indicates one of two things. It could be that she is not authentic or congruent enough to express her feelings toward the person who is in the room with her. That is, she responds in a way that she thinks will maintain the relationship with the counselor and denies that she might resent his role as helper. (Sometimes when a counselee expresses feelings about others they are also expressing those same feelings about the counselor). Or, it could be that she really does not feel the same way about the counselor as she does about others who have played the helper role in the past.

Line 30. The fact that the counselor asks the question about whether or not Sally trusts him puts her in an awkward position. She has already asserted that she does trust him (line 29). His question could even be perceived as a challenge to Sally's truthfulness. It may have been much more fruitful in terms of Sally's own self-actualization to go back to the feelings that were expressed quite powerfully in line 27.

Line 31. Now Sally seems to be aware of her present. She acknowledges that her previous experiences of trusting others have been hurtful but her current experience is not the same as her past experiences. If the counselor made a mistake in line 30, Sally uses his interpretation anyhow. She shows the self-righting capacity that leads to congruence, authenticity and self-actualization. What may (or may not) have been a mistake by the counselor is, nevertheless, used by the counselee to her own benefit. This is often the case regardless of the particular therapy used by the counselor.

Line 32. Sally's attitude about people who "help" her and the feelings that their "help" evoke are respected by the counselor. Given her response in the next line, it would seem that it is the acknowledgement by the counselor of her being hurt by those whom she has trusted in the past that opens the door for Sally's new discovery about herself.

Line 33. The counselor's unconditional positive regard for Sally provides an opportunity for her to assess her own need for independence. She has experienced his empathy and acceptance, which paved the way for her to accept his interpretation about her attitudes regarding trusting others. As a result, she becomes more congruent as her need to feel independent is recognized for what it is, a way to hide her reluctance to trust others who may hurt her.

Line 34. The counselor's empathic understanding and his unconditional positive regard for Sally do not preclude him from telling her the truth as he understands it.

Line 35. Sally may be embarrassed about her lack of independence "being discovered" which would explain her laughter.[17] This highlights an important feature of all of the talking therapies. The goal of a counseling session is not necessarily to make the counselee feel good. The goal is for the counselee to achieve mental and emotional well-being (the psychoanalytically informed therapies) or to grow and develop in her journey toward increasing congruence and self-actualization (person-centered therapy).

For the Christian counselor, however, the most important insight that Sally has gained is the one that applies to her spiritual life. She is able to speak comfortably about her need for God to love her because she knows that the Christian counselor shares her commitment to her spiritual life as part of her journey toward self-actualization.

Sally discovered that the more she knows herself from an emotional perspective, the more she learns about herself from a spiritual perspective. One's emotional life and spiritual life are closely intertwined. They are obviously not the same thing but just as the emotions lead the way to the unconscious (Freudian theories) so too do they lead the way to a better understanding of our relationship with God.

Person-Centered Therapy is widely used by Christian Counselors, in part because its basic techniques (reflective listening and unconditional positive regard) are easily acquired. While some of the assumptions from which these techniques are derived are either extra-biblical or anti-biblical, the theory does provide some useful concepts and practices that can be adopted by the Christian counselor as he/she counsels with an individual counselee.

---

[17] Could it be that the unconscious has been made conscious even though person-centered counseling is not focused on that?

Biblical and Theological Reflections

While person-centered therapy has much to recommend it, especially for the non-professional Christian counselor, some of its assumptions must be questioned in relation to the biblical teaching about what it means to be human.

Rogers' concept of individualization is extra-biblical, that is, it is not found in scripture. However, it does have a distinctly New Testament (as opposed to Hebrew Bible) connotation. Most of Jesus' teachings are directed at the individual, as are the apostle Paul's. But the Hebrew scriptures (the Old Testament) are primarily written for and to the nation of Israel. While there are beautiful writings addressed to the individual (the Proverbs are a great example), the major focus of the Hebrew Bible is on the group, Israel, rather than the individual.

Christianity has a tendency to place the individual and his/her salvation and sanctification above the interests of the family and certainly above the interests of the nation. But the idea of being a self-governing individual whose task is self-actualization may lack the balance required between the needs of the individual and that same individual's need to belong to a family and a church community.

The distinction between a highly individualistic and a highly communal perspective is particularly relevant to counselors who work with people of ethnic groups whose cultures place more emphasis on the family than on the individual. Many people from Asiatic cultures or Hispanic cultures, for example, value their membership in their family (often including the extended family) much more than they do their own individuality. When counseling with people from these cultures it cannot be assumed that good old American individualism is the healthiest or most well adjusted life-style. For people from these cultures, person-centered therapy may not be the best choice. Family therapy (Chapter VII) also recognizes the need for individualization but within the context of the family and may be more useful for those whose cultures are different from the majority of Americans.

Another important assumption of person-centered therapy is that to be human is to have an innate drive toward self-actualization. Self-actualization, according to Rogers, means that a person discovers through his/her own experiences, what is his or her own human potential and continually actualizes that potential.

The belief that we are driven toward self-actualization must be questioned for two reasons. First, the concept includes the assumption that we create ourselves anew on a continuing basis. Second, Rogers believes that self-actualization is a process that is based on a natural inclination toward goodness. These beliefs need to be compared with the teachings of scripture.

The idea that we create who we are is simply not supported by scripture. The biblical view is clear, "Train a child in the way that he should go and when he is old he will not turn from it" (Proverbs 22:6). In human history, and certainly in an individual life, the present is built upon the past. The notion that each of us is free to decide who we are at any given moment is appealing but the scriptures (and history) teach us something very different.

Many people have also criticized Rogers' understanding that human beings are basically good. Person-centered therapy is based on the assumption that to be self-actualized is to achieve the highest potential for goodness. But what if to be fully self-actualized means just the opposite? What if our innate propensity is not toward goodness but toward evil? Rogers, of course, believes that basic human nature is good so that actualizing that basic nature is to reach toward goodness.

There is much in Rogers' writing that would suggest that he does, in fact, believe that human beings are basically good. For example, he wrote "One of the most revolutionary concepts to grow out of our clinical experience is the growing recognition that the innermost core of 'man's nature,' is positive in nature - is basically socialized, forward moving, rational and realistic." (Rogers, 1995, pgs 90-91). The idea that human beings are basically "positive in nature" certainly contradicts the biblical teaching about the human condition, which is that "there is no one righteous, not even one." (Romans 3:10).

It should be noted, however, that many of those who have followed in Rogers' footsteps have questioned his understanding of human nature. They recognize that human beings do sometimes choose to be cruel, greedy, lacking in moral direction and even murderous (Gurman and Messer, 1995). Of course, we are also capable of choosing to be kind, generous, principled and loving.

This emphasis on free will, the capacity to make choices about who we are and who we want to become is highly controversial. Rogers differentiates his understanding of humanity from the Freudians by denying that we are pre-determined to be who we are by the forces that shaped us during our "formative" years. While the earlier therapies put too much emphasis on determinism, Rogers seems to have gone too far in the other direction with his insistence on free will.

What does the Bible teach us about human freedom and destiny? It is clear that Adam and Eve had free will, and they used their free will when they chose to disobey God. When they were expelled from the Garden of Eden they, and all of humanity, were cursed with specific punishments, but their free will was not taken from them or us.

But Adam and Eve were never completely free. They could not decide to breathe under water like a fish, to fly like birds or to become as tall as a giraffe. Human beings do not usually decide when to get ill or when to die. We do not decide who our biological parents are or if we will have siblings. We do not decide on our genetic makeup and we do not decide on the most important aspects of our environment. Our free will is limited by circumstances over which we have no control.

The fact is that both the Freudians and Carl Rogers have missed the mark. Human beings are free to make decisions but we are also destined to make those decisions within a given framework. For example, the child who is reared by critical and abusive parents does not have the same degree of freedom to decide to be a loving and nurturing person as does the child who has had accepting and affirming parents. The whole concept of self-actualization is based on freedom for each person to choose, but that freedom is severely curtailed by circumstances beyond our control.

We must conclude, then, that some of the major assumptions of person-centered therapy are highly questionable to say the least. But that does not mean that the therapy itself cannot be useful for the Christian counselor. There are several theoretical concepts and practical applications that are particularly appealing to Christians engaged in the ministry of counseling.

The first important concept is that of the uniqueness of each individual. This is an extra-biblical concept but a very important one. While human beings have much in common, especially those who live in a shared culture, it is the wondrous uniqueness of each counselee that should always be the focus of attention by the counselor. Theories of personality can enhance our understanding of people in general. But in the counseling session, as in all of life, the individual is unlike "people in general" in highly significant ways.

Second, the attitude of unconditional positive regard is certainly congruent with the biblical understanding of what it means to love one's neighbor. This attitude does not mean that the counselor approves of everything that the counselee says and does. What it does mean is that the counselor accepts the *human being* who says things that are cruel and behaves in ways that are immoral. It means that the counselor remembers that while he himself was still a sinner, Christ died for him. The God who accepts the sinner is present in the counselor who gives to the counselee unconditional positive regard. That is, the counselor loves the counselee the way God loves the counselor.

The third important concept of person-centered therapy is congruence, especially as it applies to the counselor. Congruence suggests that the counselor is not only well-integrated but is also capable of being authentic. She is aware of her own feelings, thoughts, prejudices, attitudes, hopes, aspirations, etc. and acts from her own genuine self rather than plays the role of counselor. The counselor who is both congruent and authentic knows herself well enough not to get in the way of the Holy Spirit's power to heal. While she may not be knowledgeable about psychological theories, the congruent and authentic counselor is knowledgeable about herself.

Hopefully, the reader will permit a very personal observation about people who want to be counselors. I have noticed that those of us who are interested in psychology and counseling have acquired that interest because we recognize in ourselves the need for emotional and spiritual healing. If this describes you, then you would be well served by engaging in a therapeutic process as a counselee before you become a counselor. Regardless of the theories that you learn and the techniques that you use, the most important tool for the counselor is himself or herself. That tool must be appropriate to the task, so counselor, know thyself.

Questions to Consider

1) Compare and contrast two basic techniques of person-centered therapy with psychoanalytic therapy. What are the advantages and disadvantages of each of these techniques?

2) Are the goals of person-centered therapy appealing to you personally? Do you believe that they are biblical, anti-biblical or extra-biblical?

3) Is the goal of self-actualization selfish? In what ways might a self-actualizing person be truly unselfish?

4) Critique the "self-righting" concept. Are there other explanations for the ability of some children to thrive in highly dysfunctional families and communities? What might some of those explanations be?

5) How do you feel about the fact that Sally (the fictitious counselee) was not encouraged to acknowledge her anger (expressed in line 27) more directly? If you had been the counselor, would you have raised it? Explain.

6) Do you agree with Rogers' belief that we live in the now and choose to be who we are?

7) What is your understanding of unconditional positive regard? Compare your understanding of the concept with the command to love our neighbors as we love ourselves. Why might such an attitude be helpful to a counselee?

REFERENCES

Gurman, A. and Messer, S. (eds.) (1995). *Essential psychotherapies: Theory and practice.* New York: Guilford Press.

Masten, A., Best, K. and Garmazy, N. (1990). Resilience and development: Contributions from the study of children who overcome adversity. *Development and Psychopathology.* 2. 425-444.

Rogers, C. (1995). *On becoming a person.* Boston: Houghton Mifflin.

Tillich, P. (1957). *Systematic Theology: Volume Two.* Chicago: University of Chicago Press.

SUGGESTED READING

Levant, R. & Shlien, J. (eds.) (1984). *Client-centered therapy and person-centered approach: New developments in theory, research and practice.* New York: Praeger.

Lietaer, G., Rombauts, J. & Van Balen, R. (eds.) (1990). *Client-centered and experiential psychotherapy in the nineties.* Belgium: Leuven University Press.

Rogers, C. (1995). *On becoming a person.* Boston: Houghton Mifflin.

CHAPTER IV
Learning To Change

The therapies already described; psychoanalytic, object relations and person-centered are all non-directive. The practitioners of these types of therapies listen to the counselee and then offer interpretations. Psychoanalysts interpret unconscious events, thoughts and motives. Practitioners of Object Relations Theory also interpret the unconscious but their focus is on how and why the individual relates to important people in his/her life. The person-centered therapist interprets by reflecting back to the counselee what she is feeling and saying.

The therapies described in this chapter take a very different approach. The practitioners of learning theory are highly directive. They are teachers rather than interpreters. Also, their concern is with the specific problem that the counselee wants to address. Greater self-understanding or an increase in self-actualization are not the goals of counseling for the learning theories and their practitioners. They want to change very specific behaviors or emotions.

Another significant difference between these types of therapies and the "talking therapies" is that the learning therapies are based on scientific evidence attained from rigorously controlled experiments. This gives the counselor as well as the counselee confidence in the methods used and feedback about the success of these methods.

While all of the learning therapies share a conviction that their methods must be scientifically verifiable, they each differ significantly in their actual practices because each is based on a different theory of learning. The three most widely accepted learning theories are; (1) operant conditioning, (2) classical conditioning and (3) modeling. Each of these theories is distinctive but they are not mutually exclusive. In fact, the counselor who is familiar with all three of the theories and their techniques will probably use all three, depending on the particular problem that he is trying to ameliorate.

For the operant conditioning theorists (sometimes called behaviorists), it is behavior that is the focus of the therapy. Emotions are often the motivation that brings a person to counseling, but they are dealt with by changing behaviors. For example, a counselee may be terrified of going to the mall (a condition known as agoraphobia). That is, the emotion of fear motivates the counselee's behavior but the focus of the behaviorist is to change what she does, not how she feels.

In applying the techniques that are designed to change behavior, the behaviorists make an important assumption. That is, that human beings learn simple tasks the same way animals do. So their experiments use rats, mice, cats and other laboratory animals.

A typical experiment using operant conditioning would be to teach a pigeon to peck at a green light. A hungry pigeon (at 80% of its normal weight) is put in a small cage. Then a green light goes on. If the pigeon pecks at the light, it is given a food pellet. Since the pigeon is hungry, the food is believed by the experimenter to be very rewarding. This procedure is repeated several times. Then a red light is flashed on alongside the green one. If the pigeon pecks at the red light there is no food pellet, if it pecks at the green light it does get the food pellet. It typically takes only a few trials for the pigeon to learn to ignore the red light and peck at the green one (Skinner, 1953).

The food pellet is called a positive reinforcement. Since it is not possible to know what the pigeon thinks, the reinforcement is considered positive because of the results that it achieves. That is, the food pellet for the pigeon is a positive reinforcement because it increases the probability that the behavior that produced the pellet will be repeated.

Positive reinforcement is a powerful technique, especially with children. Have you ever taught a young child to say please? If you have, you probably did so by offering the child something she wanted, a cookie for example. But if you didn't actually give it to her until she said please and then gave it to her immediately after she did say "the magic word," then you used a positive reinforcement. Receiving the cookie increased the probability that she would say please the next time she asked for one.

The drawback with this method is that the child has to know how to say please in the first place. Positive reinforcement doesn't teach a specific behavior, it only increases the likelihood that the behavior would be repeated.

Another important feature related to the effectiveness of positive reinforcement is that it has to be given immediately after the desired behavior. If there is a significant time-lapse between the behavior and the reinforcement, then the technique is less reliable. Generally speaking, the younger the child the shorter the amount of time there should be between the behavior and the reinforcement.

For adults, the amount of time between behavior and reinforcement can be extended considerably. How many people drag themselves out of bed, go to a job they hate and work hard at that job just to get a paycheck at the end of the week? To be sure, there are intermediate reinforcements. That cup of coffee in the morning is a reward for getting out of bed, visiting with one's co-workers once the worker arrives at his job is rewarding as well. But it's that paycheck at the end of the week that is probably the most important positive reinforcement.

So what happens if that worker makes a mistake at work? What if he accidentally breaks a machine that cost his employer a great deal of money? Then the boss is likely to reprimand him sharply in front of everyone. That is, she punishes the worker. What do scientific experiments teach us about the effects of punishment?

Under very specific conditions, punishment can temporarily decrease the probability that the punished behavior will be repeated (Skinner, 1953). Notice the distinction between punishing the behavior and punishing the person. If there is a significant time-lapse between the unwanted behavior and the punishment, then it is the person who is punished, not the behavior.

Referring again to the worker who makes a mistake on the job, if the aversive stimulus (punishment) is a natural consequence of his own behavior, then that punishment can be effective. For example, if the employee got a mild electric shock when he broke the machine, then that would be a natural consequence of his own mistake. The employee was punished and he is very unlikely to make the same mistake again. Any further punishment would be unnecessary and ineffective.

Actually, punishment administered by someone else is almost always ineffective. The worker who caused his machine to break down has already been punished. For his boss to reprimand him an hour later is not only unnecessary but also counter-productive. Why? Because instead of the worker being angry with himself he is now angry with his boss for punishing him.

That is, the punishment is associated, not with the worker's behavior but with the boss who punished him. The worker learns to dislike and avoid his boss. Whenever the boss comes near the worker, he feels afraid of her and as a result he probably performs his job less efficiently.

This example of associating a punishment with the punishing agent is a description of classical conditioning. This kind of learning is different from operant conditioning in that classical conditioning changes motivation and emotions while operant conditioning changes behaviors. The worker who associates punishment with the punishing agent has been classically conditioned to fear his boss.

Classical conditioning was first made famous by a Russian named Ivan Pavlov (Gurman and Messer, 1995). Pavlov noticed that when food is placed in front of a dog, the dog begins to salivate even before he starts to eat the food. Of course, salivation is required for digestion but the dog salivated before he started to eat. Why? Because the dog connected the mere presence of food with actually eating it. That is, the dog associates the presence of food (which did not require saliva) with the eating of the food (which did require saliva). So Pavlov wanted to find out if the dog would salivate to something other than the presence of food. Pavlov wondered if the dog would salivate to a completely neutral stimulus like the sound of a bell. In order to satisfy his curiosity, Pavlov rang a bell just before he put food in front of the dog. He did this a few times and then rang the bell without giving the dog any food. Sure enough, the dog salivated to the sound of the bell, which he had been taught, conditioned, to associate with the food (Watson, 1924).

Other scientists continued these experiments. They found that the bell could be associated with a light, a light could be associated with a person, etc. In each case the dog (or any subject) experienced what is called higher order conditioning. The original stimulus (food) could be generalized to any number of stimuli in order to evoke the response of salivation.

The fact that a natural physiological response (salivation) can be conditioned, that is trained through association, makes classical conditioning a powerful tool for manipulating human motives and emotions because they too are based on natural physiological responses. This kind of manipulation is used all the time especially by the advertising industry.

Have you ever wondered why movie stars try to sell things like medicines? The reason for a vast expenditure on highly paid actors is that most advertising is based on classical conditioning. The esteemed movie star is associated with a certain brand of medicine. Since the star is admired and respected, the same feelings are associated with the medicine that the actor is selling. The fact that this type of advertising works is a good indication that it is not only dogs that can be classically conditioned.

Back to the worker who is punished by his boss. The worker is humiliated by his boss's reprimand. He associates the boss with that painful feeling. He alternates between anger at her and fear of further humiliation. He has learned nothing at all about what behavior he needs to avoid in order to be a good worker, he has only learned that he doesn't like his boss. And through classical conditioning, as he associates his boss with his job, he hates his job as well.

A punitive boss creates further unwanted effects. As a person in authority, she is likely to be a role model for those who work for her. So they in turn will also be more critical and punitive as they imitate her, possibly without even realizing that they are doing so.

That is, they learn to model their behavior after their boss's behavior. This third type of learning theory, called modeling, is currently being used by therapists and others all over the world.

Imitating a role model is a very common phenomenon. Children copy other children as well as cartoon characters, admired athletes, etc. If you've ever watched a Little League game, you can easily tell who the batter's favorite player is because he copies that player's mannerisms at the plate.

One of the biggest concerns of many adults has been that children not only imitate their favorite sports heroes, they imitate less acceptable models as well. The adults' fear is that when children watch violent behavior on television and in the movies that they will copy that behavior (Bandura, 1969). This concern has been the topic of rigorous experimentation to see if, in fact, children really do increase their own aggressive behavior after watching others act aggressively.

What the researchers found was that their concerns were justified. Children did express more aggressive behavior after watching others' aggression. What the children saw was even more likely to be copied when positive reinforcements were given either to the model that the children watched or the children themselves who subsequently exhibited their own aggressive behavior.

These researchers also found that punishing aggressive behavior had little or no effect. As could have been predicted, once a child learned to be aggressive by imitating someone else, that behavior could be only temporarily inhibited by the use of punishment.

But children are not the only ones who imitate what they see.Adults copy other adults as well. The tennis coach shows his students how to hold the racket, what to do with the ball, how to hit it in order to win the point. His students imitate, as closely as they can, what the coach has modeled for them. Adults learn more complicated tasks through modeling as well. That's why this book includes so many fictitious counseling sessions. The verbatim accounts are presented so that the reader might imitate some of the fictitious counselor's techniques.

Modeling, operant conditioning and classical conditioning are all potentially useful for the Christian counselor. Techniques such as positive reinforcement, learning through associating an object or person with an emotion and modeling have all been shown to be effective. The application of these techniques will be illustrated in several fictitious counseling sessions, but first it may be useful to critique the theories and their techniques.

The scientific approach that is so highly valued by the learning theorists does make some profound assumptions with which the Christian counselor may not agree. Primarily, these theorists believe that each human being is born *tabula rasa*, a blank slate. Biological predispositions, innate talents or disabilities are discounted as irrelevant. All that matters in the development of a human being is what he or she has learned from the environment, including of course, the human environment.

Another concern about all of the learning theories is that they are based on the assumption that human beings are merely passive recipients of various types of conditioning. It seems very clear, however, that human beings actually make decisions based on reflection, analysis and logic. We are not like monkeys who copy whatever we see. We do not buy medicines just because a favorite actor encourages us to do so. Most people do not repeatedly engage in life-threatening acts just because the positive reinforcement of living through one was highly gratifying. We think about our decisions. We weigh the pros and cons of the consequences of our behavior. We are not machines who simply respond to whatever data has been entered into our "systems."

All of the learning theories have been justly criticized for their assumption that human beings are merely passive recipients of environmental influences. But classical conditioning has come under particular scrutiny, in part because the use of its techniques is so potentially harmful.

Classical conditioning is often used by cults who offer fellowship to lonely people as they learn of the cult's "attractions." Young people looking for a group with which to identify can be taught to associate the sense of belonging provided by the welcoming cult members with the cult leader. In order to maintain their feeling of belonging, they may follow the leader blindly and sometimes destructively.

In addition to the justified concerns about conditioning, there have also been unjustified criticisms. For example, some critics have suggested that untreated causes of specific problems simply manifest themselves in new ways after the old behaviors or emotions have been changed. There is, however, little if any scientific evidence to support this particular criticism. While it is true that the cause is not addressed, it is possible that simply changing a behavior or a specific emotion is enough to meet even the long-term needs of the counselee.

While learning theorists and those who use their theories don't deal with underlying causes, their techniques have been shown to be effective in terms of the results and the time it takes to accomplish the desired outcome, usually around six to eight sessions. This is an important consideration for the inexperienced Christian counselor for whom more than six to eight sessions is probably inappropriate.

Fictitious Counseling Session I: Operant Conditioning

The "counselor" is Susan, a high school English teacher who volunteered to teach at a vacation Bible school in an Indian Reservation. The "counselees" are a group of 12 students in fifth and sixth grade.

On the first day of vacation Bible school, the children started coming to class about a half an hour past the time designated for the class to start. Some of the students didn't arrive until more than an hour later. Susan respected the difference in cultural attitudes about timelines but she was also eager to have as much time as possible with her students. So she initiated a process known as successive approximations.

The class was supposed to start at 9:00 a. m. So Susan talked about the goal of starting on time and told her students what the plan was for achieving that goal. She told her students that on the second day, everyone who arrived by 9:30 would get a marker that glowed in the dark. On the third day, each student who arrived by 9:25 (five minutes earlier) could pick out his or her own marker. Each student who was in school by 9:15 on the following day would pick out two markers. By the second week, most of the children were in their seats by 9:15 (a compromise between Susan's need for punctuality and the students' cultural attitudes about being on time).

On that first day of school, the students were quiet and shy. But by the second day they were actively engaged in answering the teacher's questions and genuinely enthusiastic about asking their own. The problem was that they all spoke at once. No one listened to anyone else. So Susan had all of the students sit around a table. She gave each one ten nickels and then explained the game that they were about to play.

Susan would ask a question and the class would discuss the answer among themselves. But when one person was speaking, anyone who interrupted the speaker would have to give that person a nickel. After twenty minutes, each student could keep the nickels that he or she hadn't given away. It took about ten minutes for the children to stop interrupting and actually listen to each other (and keep their nickels).

By the second week of vacation Bible school, it became clear to Susan that memorizing verses from the Bible was not one of the students' favorite activities. So she made up a chart and put it where all of the students could see it. Across the top of the chart she put each child's name and along the side of the chart she listed the ten Bible verses that they were required to memorize. The students practiced saying the verses during the day and at the beginning of the next day they were asked to repeat the verse. Each child who was able to do so would see a star on the chart below his/her name next to the specific verse that was memorized.

Susan's plan didn't work. Only one or two children regularly received a star. So she talked to the students about how to change the plan in order to make it more effective. The children decided that there were two problems with the chart. First, the star on a chart was not very appealing to them. They decided that they would rather see a picture of a long house like the homes their ancestors used to live in. They also told the teacher that they wanted the picture to be put on the chart the day they learned the verse, not the following day. After these adjustments were made, most of the children learned most of the verses and could repeat them on the last day of the two-week vacation Bible school.

Analysis

This "counseling session" illustrates three major techniques of operant conditioning. The first is that of successive approximations. This technique breaks down the desired goal into small and readily achievable parts, with each successive part a little more difficult but coming closer to the desired goal. As each mini-goal is achieved (coming closer to the target of 9:15 starting time), the student received a positive reinforcement that increased the probability that the goal of coming at the required time on the next day would be achieved.[18]

Of course, the plan for getting the children to come to school on time included a relatively long interval between behavior and reinforcement. The children had to get up earlier, or walk faster, or not stop to talk to their neighbors on the way to school before they received the positive reinforcement of the marker. Instead of a few minutes, the time between getting to school at the designated time and the reinforcement upon achieving that goal could have been an hour or more.

But the marker met an intrinsic need for these students, a need that is just as real as a hungry pigeon's need for a food pellet. These children were very creative and a marker that glowed in the dark enabled them to express their innate creativity with a medium that was not readily available to them. A positive reinforcement that meets an intrinsic need[19] (*e.g.*, creative expression) is powerful enough to be effective even when there is a relatively long period of time between the desired behavior and the positive reinforcement. A reinforcement that does not meet such an intrinsic need is much less powerful and needs to be given almost immediately.

---

[18] Since the counselor is basically saying "if you do this, then I'll give you that" the positive reinforcement is also a bribe.

[19] Of course, behaviorists don't believe we have intrinsic needs, this is the author's interpretation.

The second technique that Susan used was actually a combination of punishment and positive reinforcement. When the children had to give one of their nickels to the person whom they interrupted, that was a punishment. The punishment was not too aversive because each child still had nickels left in his/her pile. Susan very wisely gave each of the students more nickels than it would take to learn to stop interrupting each other. It usually only takes three or four trials for children this age to change their behavior and they each had ten nickels. So Susan could be quite confident that each child would not only be punished for interrupting, but that each would also have a positive reinforcement for listening.

The third technique of operant conditioning that is illustrated in this case also uses positive reinforcement, but this time without punishment. The chart was intended to reinforce the memorization of Bible verses. But it did not work. It was not until the children felt that they had input into the use of the chart. They needed to be consulted and therefore empowered before they were willing to engage in the teacher's plan. Very young children do not expect to be consulted about their own behaviors. But older children are much more likely to cooperate when they are included in making up the rules that they are expected to follow.

When the teacher did involve the students in the setting up of the chart, they decided to change the reinforcement itself as well as the schedule on which it was given. These Native American children wanted their culture to be respected. They wanted to be accepted for who they are, for their unique place in American life. So they wanted a long house, not a star under their names on the chart. The children not only felt validated but in the process they taught Susan about a culture that she knew very little about. And she in turn became a better teacher.

The timing of the positive reinforcements was also a problem. Positive reinforcements must be given shortly after a specific behavior (*e.g.,* saying a verse from memory). The teacher thought that the children might practice their verses at home in order to receive a positive reinforcement the next day. But the time between practicing at home and receiving the reinforcement the following day was much too long.

Of course, the children could delay a positive reinforcement for coming to school on time. But that was because of a combination of a shorter time-lapse (an hour instead of overnight) and the appeal of the reinforcement (a marker that they could keep versus the picture of a long house on a chart that they couldn't keep).

This example of operant conditioning presents an interesting paradox. While the techniques that were used come from very reliable scientific experiments, the practitioner of those techniques must still be able to be both creative and flexible in order to use them effectively.

Fictitious Counseling Session II: Classical Conditioning

May is a sophomore at a local high school. She is intelligent, physically attractive and popular. She is active in the church youth group and attends worship services regularly. The counselor is her Sunday school teacher.

Line 1. May: Hi, are you busy?

Line 2. Counselor: No, I always have time for you.

Line 3. May: Well, my mom said I should come to talk to you because I'm having a problem at school.

Line 4. Counselor: Oh, I'm sorry to hear that. Tell me about it.

Line 5. May: Well, I'm doing pretty well in all my classes except math. I usually get what the teacher is talking about, but when it comes to taking the quizzes, I just freeze. it's like, you know, like my brain turns off. I just can't think and it's so frustrating because I really do know the stuff, you know?

Line 6. Counselor: When you say your brain turns off, what do you mean?

Line 7. May: You know, I just get so nervous.

Line 8. Counselor: I get what you mean. You know the material but you get anxious, scared when it comes time to take the test.

Line 9. May: Boy, you can say that again. My hand shakes so hard that I can hardly hold the pencil. It feels like my heart is beating so loud that every one can hear it. It's terrible.

Line 10. Counselor: I'd like to help you, are you in?

Line 11. May: Yea, I really need your help.

Line 12. Counselor: Okay, this is what we're going to do. First, we're going to make a list of the scariest things about taking a math exam. Then I'm going to teach you some relaxation techniques. After that we're going to imagine you're going through the scariest parts of taking the test while at the same time practicing the relaxation techniques that you learned. How does that sound?

Line 13. May: I'm not sure I followed all that, but lets go for it.

Line 14. Counselor: Tell me when you're least nervous, is it when the teacher tells you there's going to be a quiz or maybe when you walk into the room to take the test. You tell me, when are you least nervous?

Line 15. May: I think when he tells us there's going to be a quiz.

Line 16. Counselor: Okay, after he says there's going to be a quiz, when is the next time that you feel nervous?

Line 17. May: Well, I guess that's when I open the math book and start to study.

Line 18. Counselor: After that?

Line 19. May: That would be when I walk into the classroom to take the test.

Line 20. Counselor: Then what?

Line 21. May: I guess that's when I sit down and actually get the exam.

Line 22. Counselor: So, you first get nervous when the teacher announces a quiz, but you're not too nervous. After that you feel a little more nervous when you start to study for the quiz, then it's when you walk into the classroom and then when you actually get the quiz. Is that right?

Line 23. May: Yea, that's pretty much it.

Line 24. Counselor: It's really hard to take an exam when you're so nervous. The good news is that it's all right to be a little nervous when you take a test - it helps you to think better. But your nervousness is over the top; it is really preventing you from doing as well as you're capable of doing. So, I'm going to teach you how you can help yourself relax. Okay?

Line 25. May: Sounds good to me.

Line 26. Counselor: I'd like you to close your eyes and take some deep breaths. (*May does that*). Good, now I'd like you to imagine Jesus standing in front of you. Can you see Him smiling at you? (*May nods in agreement*). Now I want you to wiggle your toes and concentrate on relaxing all of your muscles. Can you feel your breathing slow and your heart slowing down? Now I want you to imagine that your math teacher is telling the class that there will be an important exam next Monday and he expects everyone to do well on it. Can you see Jesus smiling at you? Now He's sitting down right next to you.

(*They repeat this several times until May replaces her fear response with the relaxation she feels with a vision of Jesus sitting beside her and encouraging her. Then they practice the same technique with each of the events that make May nervous. They start with the least anxiety-producing event, which is the announcement of the exam. Then they go through the other events that May has named*).

Line 27. Counselor: Good work, May. Now, does a math exam feel so scary?

Line 28. May: No. I know that if I study hard Jesus will be with me. His presence will help me relax. I just have to keep reminding myself that He is with me always.

Analysis

Lines 1-2. The shared greeting indicates that May and the counselor already have a good relationship.

Line 3. May makes it clear that it was not her idea to see the counselor.

Line 4. The counselor is less interested in whose idea it was for May to come and more interested in the specific problem that May (or her mother) wants to address.

Line 5. May tries to describe her problem. Her description certainly points to a diagnosis of test anxiety, but it could also suggest a physical problem or a relational problem with her math teacher.

Line 6. The counselor asks for clarification by using May's own terms her "brain turns off."

Lines 7 - 9. May is able to describe her test anxiety in no uncertain terms. So once the therapeutic goal is explained to May it is clear to her that the goal really does address the problem that May has explicitly stated.

Line 10. The counselor's question "are you in" reveals a subtle change in language for the counselor. He uses the vernacular of the average adolescent as a way to connect with May.

Line 11. May's response indicates that she feels the counselor's connection, which makes her more willing to participate in whatever the counselor suggests as a solution to her problem.

Lines 12 - 23. The counselor lists each event that leads to May's anxiety. It is important to note that the closer May comes to actually taking the exam the more nervous she becomes. This information is important because the relaxation response will work better with low-anxiety events and can then be used as the higher-anxiety events are encountered. To begin with the highest-anxiety event could result in a failure to actually achieve a significant relaxation response and May might give up on the whole process.

Lines 24 - 25. The counselor explains that feeling a little anxious can actually be helpful when taking an exam. Physiologically, anxiety at an optimal level makes us more alert and more focused. The counselor assures May that she doesn't need to feel nervous about feeling a little nervous when faced with taking a math quiz.

Lines 26 - 27. The relaxation response that the counselor teaches May is similar to one that was devised decades ago by a doctor who used it for his patients with heart disease (Benson, 1975). Although the technique did not originally include a vision of Jesus, many people do use mental images to help them relax.

May learns to associate, through classical conditioning, an anxiety-provoking event with the physical response of relaxation. Just as the dog salivated (a physiological response) when he ate his food and then salivated when he heard a bell by associating that with food, so too May's physiological response (relaxation) becomes associated with a particular event (announcement of an exam).

Line 28. May has learned so much more than how to pass a math test. She has learned how to put her faith into action. There is good reason to believe that she will continue to look to her faith to support her when life requires her to face even greater challenges than test anxiety.

Fictitious Counseling Session III: Modeling

Ian is a rather small thirteen-year-old boy. He seems very shy. He comes to the counseling session with his mother, Sarah, who does most of the talking. The counselor is the pastor of a church. Sarah and Ian do not attend his church but a friend suggested that Sarah should go and talk to him.

Line 1. Sarah: Hi, thank you for seeing us.
Line 2. Counselor: You're welcome. Who's going to tell me what brings you?
Line 3. Sarah: There are three or four bullies at Ian's school who call him names. They trip him in the halls and a few days ago they even threw him in a gym locker and left him there until a janitor finally heard him banging on the locker. This has got to stop. So I told the principal what happened and he said there was nothing he could do, he just said that boys will be boys. I know that the only way for Ian to end this bullying is for him to fight back, but he doesn't like to fight, he just won't stand up for himself.
Line 4. Counselor: Ian?
Line 5. Ian: They're bigger than me, what can I do when they all gang up on me (*crying*)?
Line 6. Counselor: What can I do for you?
Line 7. Sarah: I want you to teach him to stand up for himself.
Line 8. Counselor: Ian, is that what you'd like to do?
Line 9. Ian: I guess.
Line 10. Counselor: Good. What are you doing tomorrow after school?
Line 11. Ian: Nothin' I guess.
Line 12. Counselor: How would you like to come with me to

the church league basketball game? But before you answer, there's a catch. I'd like to take you to the game, but then you have to play at our team's next practice. The coach and I are friends so I know it will be okay. How about it?

Line 13. Ian: Yeah (*excitedly*) I'd like that.

Line 14. Counselor (*to Sarah*): I'd like Ian to watch boys his own age, or a little older guarding the ball as other boys try to take it away. Then I want him to actually do what he saw the other boys do. (*To Ian*) every time you stand up for yourself on the basketball court, every time one of the other players tries to get the ball from you and you don't let him, I'm going to mark that down. And if you have three marks, then mom and you and I are going out for an ice cream to talk about how it felt when you didn't let the other boys push you around.

Analysis

Line 2. It might have been assumed that mom would do most of the talking given Ian's apparent shyness. But the counselor makes no assumptions and invites either Sarah or Ian to describe the problem that brings them for counseling.

Line 3. Sarah's description of what is happening to Ian is all too common. Bullying can have a traumatic effect on young people, if not physically then certainly emotionally. And the effect can be long lasting, so that even as an adult Ian could be shy and fearful and the victim of more subtle types of bullying.

Line 4. The counselor looks for Ian's input. He wants to be sure that this is not just Sarah's problem but that Ian sees it as his problem - a problem that he needs to address.

Line 5. Ian's tears indicate that he feels helpless and that he would find it very difficult to stand up for himself. In addition to his small size, his personality may also invite bullying.

Lines 6 - 9. Ian is certainly unhappy about his situation, but it is his mother who is even more so. It is she who demands a change.

Lines 10 - 14. The counselor wants to provide a way to accomplish the goal that Ian's mother has stated and Ian has reluctantly agreed to. That is, that Ian needs to be more assertive in protecting himself from bullies. Watching appropriate assertiveness on the basketball floor, imitating that behavior and then having that behavior reinforced (with ice cream) will probably effect significant changes in Ian. Since children imitate the aggressive behavior they see on television, why not the appropriately aggressive behavior of a basketball game?

Biblical and Theological Reflections

The three types of conditioning/learning illustrated in the preceding cases may evoke very different responses from the Christian counselor. Each will be dealt with separately because the possible objections to each are very different.

As for operant conditioning, its discouragement of punishment may seem anti-biblical to some. The Hebrew Bible in particular is filled with threats of punishments for disobeying God's commandments (*e.g.,* Deuteronomy 32: 19-42). Regarding punishment of children, we read in Proverbs that if we spare the rod we spoil the child (Proverbs 13:24). [20] But scientific evidence clearly shows that using the rod is an ineffective tool. The rod is associated with the person who uses it rather than with the behavior that prompted its use. As a result, the child learns to avoid the punisher but not necessarily to decrease the occurrence of the punished act.[21] The child may also learn that he is bad rather than what he *did* was unacceptable. In addition, the parent who uses the rod becomes so powerful that the child may learn to be who the parent wants him to be and may grow up not knowing who he really is. The child will lack congruence.

The evidence supporting the ineffectiveness of physical punishment that is sometimes used to "discipline" children (and

---

[20] When the child cries and the punishment stops, the child has received a negative reinforcement. Like positive reinforcement, it increases the probability that the preceding behavior will increase. So all that the child has learned is that when he cries he can stop the punishment.

[21] In most states physical punishment may also be illegal as well as ineffective.

sometimes adults) is quite overwhelming. But mild, non-physical punishment can temporarily inhibit inappropriate behavior as long as the desired behavior is quickly followed by a positive reinforcement.

While there is a fundamental disagreement between scripture and science regarding the physical punishment of children, there is little argument regarding the use of positive reinforcement. Scientific experiments with animals and human beings have shown positive reinforcement to be a very powerful technique in changing behavior. And the Bible also recognizes the value of rewards, although there is a difference between rewards and positive reinforcement.

Rewards are often mentioned in the Bible (*e.g.,* Deuteronomy 11: 13-32 and James 1:12). But positive reinforcement is not the same as God's promise of rewards. Positive reinforcement is given for a specific behavior, a reward is given in response to the entire life of an individual or nation. Once this distinction is recognized, the difference between reward and positive reinforcement becomes clearer.

Rewards are not given for *specific behaviors*, they are given for the way a person lives his or her life, and the Christian's commitment to Jesus Christ. Positive reinforcements are teaching tools, not rewards. Fortunately, rewards and positive reinforcement are not mutually exclusive. Parents, teachers, counselors and others may use positive reinforcement without negating the power of a heavenly reward for a godly life.

There is no disagreement, then, between the Bible and science when it comes to positive reinforcement.They do not agree, however, about the nature of humanity. Specifically, the assumption of the learning theorists that we are each born like a blank slate is not what scripture teaches. The Bible teaches that there is a certain quality known as human nature. That is, we are innately spiritual beings who were created in order to relate to God.[22] That is the essence of human nature. To say that there is no such thing as human nature contradicts the theological understanding that it is the nature of humanity that despite our

---

[22] This assertion will be discussed more fully in Chapter IX.

human inclination to sin, we seek a relationship with a loving God who has redeemed us from the power of sin and death.

Another issue that applies to both operant conditioning and classical conditioning is that both schools of thought are based on animal studies. When psychologists study animals in order to understand and control human behavior, they are assuming that humans have evolved from animals. They accept the teachings of evolution. Committed Christians disagree about the relationship between scripture and evolution and this is not the place for an in-depth discussion of that issue. Christian counselors will have to decide for themselves if the Theory of Evolution is anti-biblical and if so, does that negate the usefulness of the techniques that are derived from psychological theories that are based on animal studies.

The use of classical conditioning also presents some biblical/theological problems that are specific to this theory.The argument is sometimes made that if we relied on our faith more fully, then we would always be joyful and we would never feel afraid or anxious. And there is scriptural evidence that supports this argument. We are told, for example, to *rejoice* in adversity (Philippians 4:4), not to be *anxious* (Matthew 6:34), not to be *jealous* or *envious* (Galatians 5:19-21). These are all emotions. The fact that we are told to feel a certain way and not to feel other ways suggests that we are capable of doing so without the use of modern theories like classical conditioning.

But our faith is not always sufficient to meet the requirements of these biblical injunctions. The Christian counselor could have told Ian of God's promise to fear not because God is always with him or reminded May of Jesus' exhortation to be anxious for nothing. That however, would have been the height of insensitivity and probably totally ineffective.

Sometimes human beings are overwhelmed by powerful emotions like sadness or anxiety or grief or any other genuine feeling. To tell a person that he/she can and must get over a certain feeling because the Bible tells us to be anxious for nothing or rejoice in all things is not unlike telling someone that he/she is not allowed to sneeze, which, like emotions, is a natural physiological reaction to a stimulus.[23] The Christian counselor can teach people how to ameliorate or control strong feelings rather than lay down the law that they must not feel the way they do.

The third theory, modeling, is probably the least objectionable of all of the learning theories because it definitely is encouraged in scripture. Parents should be a good example to their children, pastors must be a good example to their parishioners, etc. The introduction of positive reinforcement (as opposed to rewards), however, is extra-biblical. The Christian counselor must decide if this extra-biblical technique is acceptable and/or useful in ameliorating human suffering.

Questions to Consider

1) Try this experiment. Ask a friend if he would participate in a scientific study. If your friend agrees, ask him to just say whatever word pops into his mind for one minute. Set a timer for 60 seconds and then say "go." For the first thirty seconds, simply record with a hash mark the number of words the person says but use a longer hash mark for every word that begins with an "s" sound. For the second thirty seconds, continue the same way you did during the first half but quietly say "mhmm" every time your friend says a word that begins with an "s" sound. Then calculate the percentage of "s" words before and then after the positive reinforcement, which was you saying "mhmm." Did your friend say a higher percentage of "s" words after you introduced the positive reinforcement? If so, was he aware that you had changed his behavior? What does this tell you about the power of positive reinforcement?

---

[23] Emotions are, for the most part, physiological. When one feels afraid or angry, for example, the heart, lungs, gastro-intestinal system, etc. are all affected. This physiological arousal is then labeled as a specific emotion (Schachter and Singer, 1962).

2) Does the research showing the ineffectiveness of punishment convince you?

3) Think of a typical example of classical conditioning. What physiological response is changed by associating it with a neutral stimulus?

4) Give three examples of individuals who model their behavior after someone else. What kind of positive reinforcements are given for that person's behavior?

5) What is your own attitude about theories that are based on an acceptance of Evolutionary Theory? If you reject a theory on the basis that it is not biblical, how do you feel about the techniques that are based on that theory?

REFERENCES

Bandura, A. (1969). *Principles of behavior modification.* New York: Holt, Rinehart and Winston.

Benson, H. (1975). *The relaxation response.* New York: Morrow.

Gurman, A. and Messer, S. (1995). *Essential Psychotherapies: Theory and Practice.* New York: Guilford Press.

.... *Holy Bible: New International Version* (1984) East Brunswick, NJ: International Bible Society.

Schachter, S. and Singer, J. (1962). Cognitive, social and physiological determinants of emotional state. *Physiological Review. 69,* 379-99.

Skinner, B. (1953). *Science and human behavior.* New York: Free Press.

Watson, J. (1924). *Behaviorism.* New York: Norton.

SUGGESTED READING

Bandura, A. (1969). *Principles of behavior modification.* New York: Holt, Rinehart and Winston.

Goldfried, M. & Davison, G. (1976). *Clinical behavior therapy.* New York: Holt, Rinehart and Winston.

Skinner, B. (1953). *Science and human behavior.* New York: Free Press.

Spiegler, M & Guevremont, D. (1993). *Contemporary behavior therapy.* Pacific Grove, CA.: Brooks/Cole.

Watson, J. (1924) *Behaviorism.* New York: Norton.

CHAPTER V
Changing How We Think:
Cognitive Therapy

Cognitive therapy deals primarily with how and what people think. It is based on some important assumptions that differ significantly from those of earlier theories. First, cognitive therapy assumes that we are proactive when thinking about ourselves, others and the world in general We are not merely passive recipients of information from our environment. We are not blank slates, nor are we are necessarily driven by unconscious motives. We encounter life and actively interpret it rather than just wait for life to make us who we are.

We not only proactively encounter life we also have the innate ability to adapt to the inevitable changes that occur in every person's life. This ability to adapt to life is at the very heart of cognitive therapy. When that natural ability becomes less than optimal, the techniques that come from the theory are intended to change thoughts that are not adaptive, that are maladaptive.

As this overview of cognitive therapy indicates, it is very different from the theories that preceded it.Nevertheless, cognitive therapy uses techniques from all of its predecessors. While the focus of cognitive therapy is on the maladaptive ways in which we think, it also recognizes the importance of emotions and behaviors, it uses behavioral techniques, it seeks to discover and make known unconscious thoughts and it values the therapeutic relationship that depends on an empathic, authentic and congruent counselor.

The therapies that together are known as cognitive therapies began making their mark in the 1960's. One of the earliest types of cognitive therapy was the Rational Emotive Therapy of Albert Ellis (Ellis, 1973). This therapy posited a cause and effect relationship between Antecedent events (A), Beliefs, (B) and Consequences (C). Ellis believed that antecedent events (A) are learned behaviors. These behaviors are then associated with irrational beliefs (B) that result in certain consequences (C) that become new antecedent events in a relatively closed circle of interactions.

For example, a person might habitually drive too fast (antecedent event). He believes that he is such an expert driver that he can avoid accidents regardless of how fast he drives (belief). He eventually has a serious car accident (consequence) but drives even faster in order to avoid other drivers who "cause" accidents (the consequence becomes an antecedent event).

Ellis's rather deterministic theory, like the behavioral theories that preceded his, left little room for the active participation of the individual in his own decisions. So his theory fails to recognize humanity's innate capacity for being proactive, which is a major assumption of the cognitive therapies that followed. But Ellis' emphasis on beliefs as a mediating factor between events and consequences was influential in the development of the cognitive therapies that followed.

Another early example of cognitive therapy was a theory that dealt primarily with depression. Several psychologists noted that for many patients depression was strongly related to maladaptive thought patterns. For example, people suffering from depression believed that they were helpless to change themselves or their world (Seligman, 1975). In addition, depressed patients only paid attention to events that were painful for them and they tended to blame themselves when things turned out badly, even when they had little or no control over those events. Perhaps most importantly, depressed patients were highly punitive of themselves while at the same time they failed to acknowledge their own acceptable behaviors and successful outcomes (Beck, 1963).

These studies of depressed patients focused on thoughts and

belief systems. So the therapies used to treat depression set about to try to change those maladaptive thoughts and beliefs. That is, psychologists moved away from the deterministic model of behavioral therapy and moved toward a model in which the individual exercised more control over his own thoughts. The extensive experimental evidence that supports the need to change cognitive processes in depressed patients is one of the reasons that it is being used so widely more than four decades later.

Cognitive therapy is not only based on experimental evidence, it also has the advantage of its practice being closely scrutinized by researchers using sophisticated statistical and experimental methodologies. Unlike the psychodynamic therapies, the outcomes of this type of therapy can be easily measured with valid and reliable psychological tests and, for the most part, the experimental evidence is very encouraging. In fact, in the treatment of depression it is the therapy of choice (along with medications where needed) for most psychologists.

For the non-professional Christian counselor, as long as a depressed counselee is being treated with appropriate medications (if needed), cognitive therapy can be a very useful tool. In order to understand the therapy well enough to use it effectively, however, it is necessary to know; (1) what is meant by the term cognition, (2) one of the guiding principles of the therapy, (3) its foundational concepts and (4) some of its techniques.

Cognition is a process that includes emotions, imagination, memory, fantasy, attitudes and goals for the future. The essence of cognition is that it involves learning and adapting. Cognition is idiosyncratic (specific to each individual), proactive and goal directed. It includes unknown assumptions and explicitly stated facts and beliefs. Cognition encompasses religious faith and scientific inquiry, illusions and delusions. It is an essential element of what it means to be human. This then, is cognition. The next step is to have at least a basic understanding of how it works.

The process of cognition begins with sensation, which is the process of sending specific types of energy from the sensory organs to the brain. This energy is then organized in the brain into meaningful information, that is, it is perceived. Once perception has taken place, some of the information moves to higher-order parts of the brain so that perceptions become thoughts that may or may not be remembered.

For example, when the eyes see a red light, photic energy is sent to the brain (sensation) where it is perceived to be a signal to stop. This perception initiates a decision-making process (thought) about what to do. Some thoughts are then stored in short-term memory and may then be stored in long-term memory. At different points in this process, the information is associated with feelings and behaviors.

This description of cognition will hopefully provide a basis for understanding one of cognitive therapy's guiding principles, which is that our understandings of our world, ourselves and our future are intricately intertwined in what has been called a cognitive triad.

One part of the cognitive triad is the world.How an individual thinks about the world is a major factor in his/her ability to adapt to the world. Are we capable of adapting our thoughts so that they become more attuned to reality and less influenced by our own subjective interpretations of the world around us? Are we open to new experiences, to new information that may contradict our previous understanding of the world? If so, then our understanding of the world will have a positive influence on our understanding of ourselves, the second part of the cognitive triad.

Once we are capable of self-reflection we tend to think a great deal about ourselves. Of course, the process of thinking about oneself is greatly influenced by how we think about the world. While it is essential for each individual to be a self who is separate and distinct from the world, it is equally important to recognize that how we perceive and understand the world has a profound affect on how we perceive and understand ourselves. For example, if we see our world as chaotic and uncontrollable, then we are likely to see ourselves as helpless in relation to such a world. On the other hand, if we see the world as orderly and largely beneficent, then we will probably see ourselves as willing participants in it.

The third part of the cognitive triad is the future. Human beings are perhaps alone in our ability to think about a time that has not yet come, that is neither past nor present. But the ability to think about and make plans for the future can be either a blessing or a curse. If the world is thought to be a dangerous place and the self is believed to be incompetent and therefore unable to deal with the world, then the future will seem very bleak. If the world is believed to be a place of opportunity despite potential dangers and the self is believed to be competent to meet whatever challenges may be presented, then the future will be embraced with hope and optimism.

Together; world, self and the future form the cognitive triad. There is typically a significant similarity in the thought patterns that relate to these three aspects of an individual's life, as the previous descriptions have already intimated. For example, when people are depressed they are usually quite pessimistic. They think more about their own personal failures than they do about their successes (self), they perceive other people as critical or selfish or condescending (world) and they have little or no hope that tomorrow will be any better than today (future). They have self-defeating thoughts and these thoughts pervade every aspect of their lives. Changing these pervasive and maladaptive thoughts requires an understanding of how they were formed in the first place. So we turn our attention to the foundational concept of cognitive therapy - the schema (the plural form is schemata).

Basically, a schema is a mental structure (metaphorically speaking) that organizes perceptions, beliefs, behaviors and emotions. A schema is formed by taking in information through a process of assimilation. This information then changes an already existing schema through a process of accommodation. That is, when new information is incorporated into an old schema that schema needs to change.

This process is illustrated when, for example, someone buys a new couch and then has to move the furniture in the living room to put the new furniture in the best place. This person assimilated a new couch into her living room, then she had to change the old furniture in order to accommodate the new couch. The new couch in the old living room is analogous to the assimilation and accommodation that take place in the development of each schema.

As essential as schemata are for adapting to life they can also be unhelpful if they do not remain fluid. Most schemata are formed during the first few decades of life. If they cannot accommodate to new information for the rest of a person's life, then they block new information from being assimilated and the old schemata become the "givens" of life. Adjusting to new circumstances and new people then becomes difficult if not impossible and thinking may become distorted.

Sometimes experiences can lead to emotions and memories that result in schemata that are maladaptive. For example, a man who has been abused as a child could develop a schema that assimilates information about cruelty and fails to assimilate information about kindness. His schema may be adaptive in relation to the abusing parent but is maladaptive in relation to potential friends or even a spouse. Because the "cruel" schema is so emotionally charged, and so limited in its capacity to assimilate kindness it fails to accommodate to new people and new circumstances.

When schemata become maladaptive they can become like self-fulfilling prophecies. Using the example of a man who had been abused as a child, he believes that people in general are cruel. As a result he relates to everyone he knows as if they would eventually inflict great pain on him. Such a person is likely to ignore acts of kindness and focus solely on *perceived* insults and rejection. He is angry with everyone whom he believes will eventually mistreat him and his hostility will invite abuse.[24]

It is not uncommon for people with maladaptive schemata to be convinced that other people treat them badly. They are likely to tell a counselor that they feel like they're walking around with a sign on their forehead that says "abuse me." They are more aware of the way others treat them than they are of their own maladaptive schemata.

As this example indicates, sometimes schemata become maladaptive, that is they become distorted. These cognitive distortions are the focus of cognitive therapy. Fortunately, sometimes just being made aware of these distortions is enough for the counselee to change them. For those that require additional

---

[24] This description would certainly apply to the fictitious person, Jenny, in Chapter II. The terminology is very different, but both theories explain the same phenomenon.

treatment there are specific techniques that will be described shortly.

Perhaps the most common cognitive distortion is dichotomous thinking, which is the belief that everything is either one way or another and there can be no middle ground. "Either I'm right or I'm wrong, not a little bit of both" is a typical example of this kind of thinking.

Another common distortion is mind reading. This involves interacting with others on the basis of what one believes the other person is thinking. This is especially maladaptive when the belief about what the other is thinking is based on one's own understanding of the world, self and the future (the cognitive triad) rather than on the person with whom one is interacting.

Another example of a cognitive distortion is selective abstraction. The person who thinks in these terms takes information from a whole body of information and selects that which "proves" what he or she already knows. For example, the man who goes to church believing that the church is all about getting money, will only remember the offertory when he leaves.

Some counselees treat a feeling as if it is a thought. In order to deal with that particular cognitive distortion, the counselor might teach the counselee the difference between feeling and thinking. For example, the counselor may take note of the way in which the counselee expresses her "feeling" by adding the word "that." A person *believes* that … but a person simply *feels* a specific emotion. She may feel afraid (end of sentence). But she believes *that* something bad is about to happen. Feelings are not easily changed, but when the counselee understands that her feeling is actually a thought, then change is more easily accomplished.

Cognitive therapy is not only interested in maladaptive thoughts, it is also interested in maladaptive but habitual thought processes. One of the most common and debilitating processes is rehearsing. Some people tend to go over and over specific events that have caused them unhappiness. In order to change this self-defeating process, the cognitive therapist would teach them to substitute more adaptive thoughts as a substitute for the maladaptive ones.

For example, instead of a counselee reminding herself over and over again about a hurtful conversation with a colleague, the counselor might instruct her to say to herself "I forgive you" every time the hurtful conversation comes to mind. It is not enough to simply tell the counselee that she must stop thinking certain things, she must find an adaptive substitute.

Related to the process of rehearsing certain events is the habit of negative self-talk, which also takes place in the person's head. People with this cognitive habit often say denigrating things about themselves to themselves. These thoughts can be even more destructive than being criticized by someone else, if only because they occur more often. The person might avoid people who are unkind and critical, but he has not learned how to avoid his own self-deprecating and self-defeating thoughts.

Like people who rehearse certain events, it is often helpful to encourage the counselee to find a positive replacement for self-deprecating thoughts. For example, the person might decide that he will replace "boy, I'm a complete loser" with "I know I can do better." It is not enough to suggest that the counselee simply stop thinking critical thoughts, they are so habitual that they must be replaced with something more positive and realistic.

Another way to change a belief or habitual way of thinking is to assign homework. A typical homework assignment would be to keep a journal in which the counselee records his or her thoughts and the specific behaviors and feelings that accompany those thoughts. A person who believes that something bad will happen to her, for example, would be required to keep a record of the specific situations in which that thought occurs, what she is doing at the time and how she is feeling when the thought comes to her.

At each session the counselor and counselee will discuss these homework assignments and sometimes they will actually practice the behaviors that the counselee must engage in. For example, if the counselee is convinced that she is going to be fired every time her employer comes near her, the counselor will play the part of the employer and the counselee will be herself. She might be instructed to say a friendly "hello" to her boss/counselor instead of avoiding him. Then the counselor and counselee might switch roles. The counselee will then be told to reflect on the role-play. How did she feel when she played each part?

The technique of fantasized consequences is also used by cognitive therapists, especially with people who are afraid to make decisions. The counselor asks the counselee to actually put into words what she thinks will happen if she makes a wrong decision. (This technique was used with Elizabeth in Chapter II). Often, once the counselee actually hears herself verbalize her fears she recognizes how unrealistic they really are. This allows her to act instead of worry about the outcome of her actions.

As these techniques indicate, the counselor plays a very active role in relation to the counselee. The counselor points out and explains the counselee's cognitive distortions. He may then prescribe specific behaviors that contradict her distortions and might give specific homework assignments. The counselor's prescriptions are then evaluated along with the counselee's adherence to those prescriptions.

One of the reasons that counselees are likely to follow the prescriptions of the professional psychologist is that the psychologist uses formal testing procedures. Psychologists will have access to very reliable psychological tests in order to identify the specific cognitive distortions of a particular counselee. Those who are not professional psychologists would not have access to those tests.

However, while the tests are useful they may not be essential. The counselor who listens closely to the counselee will learn to identify many of the cognitive distortions that the counselee suffers from. But administering psychological tests accomplishes another more subtle goal. The person who gives and interprets the test is perceived by the counselee to be an expert. When the counselor is perceived to be an expert the counselee is far more likely to follow his directions. The lack of the status of expert is exacerbated for the Christian counselor who does not receive payment for his or her services.

Another disadvantage for counselors who are not psychologists is the amount of time that is usually required for cognitive therapy. Typically the course of therapy is twelve to fifteen sessions. This is a much shorter period of time than other therapies might require but exceeds the number of sessions (six to eight) recommended for the non-professional counselor. However, if just a few cognitive distortions are focused on and the counselee is obviously making progress in changing those distortions, then the general rule of six to eight sessions need not be written in stone.

In addition to the problem of the number of sessions that may be required, there is another shortcoming in cognitive therapy. It will probably not be useful until or unless the counselee is ready to take a rational approach to his/her problems. Most people talk to a counselor because they are unhappy - not because they're not thinking appropriately. Before the counselor deals with cognitive distortions or self-defeating cognitive habits, the sensitive counselor will probably need to address the counselee's emotional issues. That is, the counselor may need to use the techniques associated with the talking therapies described in earlier chapters.

In the following fictitious counseling session, the counselor and counselee focus on cognitive distortions and those distortions are certainly associated with painful feelings. The counselee is not so distraught, however, than she needs to deal with those feelings before she addresses her maladaptive thoughts. It should be noted that some of the techniques described earlier are not used in this session. The counselor does not follow through with homework assignments or practice sessions with the counselee, nor is there a final assessment of the process. The follow-up may come when the counselee continues to work with the counselor after this first session.

Fictitious Counseling Session

Carol is a morbidly obese woman in her mid-thirties. She is not married. She is quite active in her church but has recently stopped going to choir rehearsals. The choir director is the counselor.

Line 1. Counselor *(meeting Carol in the church hallway)*: Hi Carol. How are you?

Line 2. Carol: Oh, hi. Well, I'm pretty good. But I've missed going to choir.

Line 3. Counselor: What's the problem?

Line 4. Carol: Well, I don't know.

Line 5. Counselor: Would you like to sit down for a minute and talk about what's bothering you? (*Carol nods so the counselor leads her to an empty Sunday school room).*

Line 6. Carol: I know I should go to choir, everyone thinks I should.

Line 7. Counselor: You should because *everyone thinks* you should?

Line 8. Carol: Don't you think I should?

Line 9. Counselor: Only if you want to.

Line 10. Carol: I'd like to sing in the choir, but you know…

Line 11. Counselor: No, I don't know.

Line 12. Carol: There are just so many steps up to the choir room. I really need to lose some weight. I have no energy for anything, I can't go places that I'd like to go because it means too much walking. I know that if I lost some weight I'd be so much better off.

Line 13. Counselor: You'd like to lose some weight.

Line 14. Carol: Yes, I really would but I'd have to lose so much and it would take forever and I know I just can't stick to a diet.

Line 15. Counselor: How do you know that you just can't stick with a diet?

Line 16. Carol: I just have too much weight to lose.

Line 17. Counselor: And you have to lose it in what, a day, a week, a month?

Line 18. Carol: It would probably take a year or more to lose all that I have to lose.

Line 19. Counselor: A year is a long time to stay on a diet. How long could you stay on a diet?

Line 20. Carol: Well, when I was in high school I lost 20 pounds in a couple of months.

Line 21. Counselor: So you can stay on a diet for a couple of months.

Line 22. Carol: Yea, but that was then and this is now. Twenty pounds would just be a drop in the bucket. It's not even worth it.

Line 23. Counselor: So if you can't do it all you won't even try to lose some.

Line 24. Carol: That sounds kind of dumb, doesn't it?

Line 25. Counselor: Well, I wouldn't put it quite like that but it does sound pretty self-defeating.

Line 26. Carol: Every time I've tried to go on a diet, I fail. I know that I just can't do it.

Line 27. Counselor: I thought you said that you lost weight when you were in high school.

Line 28. Carol: Well… Yes, I did. And I felt a lot better about myself when I did. *(Long pause).* You know, I think I might be able to do it again if I change my attitude. Would you be willing to talk to me again?

Line 29. Counselor: Good, I'd really like to work with you. When is a good time for you?

Analysis

Line 1. The counselor avoided a mistake that is common among churchgoers. He did not say "I've missed you at choir." That simple statement is often perceived as a rebuke, which then puts the other person on the defensive.

Lines 2 - 4. Because Carol felt the counselor's concern rather than a rebuke, she gives a very subtle hint that she would not object to talking to him.

Line 5. Christian counseling doesn't have to take place in an office. The setting could be at church (a Sunday school room) or in a home, a hospital or other institutional setting. The Christian counselor's "office" is wherever there are people in need.

Line 6. The first cognitive distortion is mind reading. Carol believes that she knows what other people are thinking, that they expect her to faithfully attend choir rehearsals.

Line 7. The counselor simply emphasizes Carol's own words so that she can think about them. There is no need to name the cognitive distortion or to lecture Carol about thinking differently or the consequences that such a change of thinking would elicit.

Lines 8 - 9. Carol focused on "should" and may have been surprised that the counselor didn't share the same opinion so she asks him about that. He very wisely and simply points out a more adaptive way of thinking - not what others might (or might not) expect but what does Carol want to do.

Line 10. Carol seems to expect that the counselor knows what she is thinking without putting her thoughts into words.

Line 11. The counselor might have taken a guess about what Carol was thinking in order to display his own empathy and perceptiveness but he gently conveys the message that neither he nor Carol can ever get inside the mind of another in order to know his/her thoughts.

Lines 12 - 13. At first Carol was a little reluctant to talk about why she was no longer able to sing in the choir (line 2) but the counselor's empathy and authenticity encouraged her to talk about herself in a very honest and courageous manner.

Line 14. Carol claims that losing weight would take forever. This obvious exaggeration, which is a cognitive distortion keeps Carol from even trying to lose at least a few pounds. She also believes that she would not be perfect in her efforts to lose weight. This too is a common cognitive distortion - dichotomous thinking. Either a task must be accomplished with perfection, or it should not even be started.

Lines 15 - 21. The counselor invites Carol to engage with him in some Socratic dialogue, questioning her belief that she cannot succeed at losing any weight at all. This is an effective technique of cognitive therapy because it engages Carol in questioning her own cognitive distortions.

Line 22. Apparently Carol recognized that her belief that she was not capable of dieting and losing weight was incorrect so she turns again to dichotomous thinking. The content of that distortion is that either she must get to a perfect weight or there is no use in even trying.

Lines 23 - 25. Carol is open to reflecting on her own cognitive distortions, perhaps because of the counselor's minimal responses. He mostly just repeats Carol's words back to her.

Lines 26 - 27. When Carol returns to her previous thinking the counselor confronts her. To be caring and empathic does not mean that the counselor cannot also be confrontational.

Line 28. Carol looked to her past experience of losing weight and her current attitude that prevents her from doing so again. Then she looked to the future and asked for the counselor's help.

Line 29. The counselor gave her a positive reinforcement ("good") for her change in thinking and made an appointment on the spot. It is not beyond the realm of possibility that in six to eight sessions, Carol may be able to change her cognitive distortions and make some real changes in her life.

Biblical and Theological Reflections

Carol seems to have conflicting beliefs. She believes that her life would be better if she lost weight but she also believes that she cannot lose even a few pounds. The presence of conflicting beliefs is especially relevant for the Christian counselor because they are such an important part of the Christian experience.

Like Carol, many persons of faith also have two competing belief systems. They have one belief system that is biblical, which promotes spiritual, religious, moral and communal well-being. They also have competing beliefs that promote none of these.

A healthy religious belief system usually consists of what we learn in Sunday school and church, our reading of scripture and our own interpretations of scripture. This belief system, however, may or may not be the one that actually guides our behaviors and informs our attitudes.

In addition to our stated beliefs, we also have unstated beliefs that are much more likely to influence how we actually live our lives. For example, most Christians believe that we are to forgive those who have sinned against us. We repeat the Lord's Prayer on a regular basis and in doing so we ask God to forgive us our debts *as we also have forgiven our debtors* (Matthew 6:12). If asked, we would no doubt state that forgiving others is an essential requirement of the Christian life. But...

We live in a world in which forgiveness is not part of our everyday thinking. Nor is it a part of our everyday experience. The basic teachings of Christianity come into conflict with the attitudes of the world with which we interact on a regular basis. Christianity requires that we forgive our neighbors but the world teaches us to get even - to get revenge. The two spheres of influence in which we live have competing messages and all too often we choose the way of the world.

The great advantage of cognitive therapy is that it can address these two competing belief systems. When, for example, someone says that she is a Christian, and then spews out nothing but vitriolic gossip about a neighbor who has hurt her, the cognitive therapist may choose to contrast her two belief systems As a Christian, this woman believes that she must forgive her neighbor, but the belief system that actually guides her behavior stands in stark contrast to those professed beliefs.When faced with this obvious contradiction, the angry Christian must make a decision. She must either forgive her neighbor or recognize that she is not the Christian that she thought she was.

As this example illustrates, scripture and cognitive therapy are very compatible. Both can be useful in changing ungodly and/or self-defeating thinking into belief systems that are in accordance with God's commandments. Of all the therapies, cognitive therapy can be used by the Christian counselor without religious concerns about its practices.

In fact, the principles of cognitive therapy can also be applied to the believer's understanding of scripture. When Christians read the Bible we often do not agree on the meaning of certain passages. Research into cognitive processes provides a means of understanding why so many people disagree so vehemently about too many issues.

When we read scripture we do so with our own prejudices. Long before we can listen to and understand the teachings of the Bible, each person has formed schemata into which the biblical teachings are assimilated. These schemata are not exclusively rational; they include emotions, behaviors and memories of events that accompany the processes that form schemata. If the schemata are too rigid, if they do not accommodate because of emotional associations, then one's interpretation of scripture may be informed by one's own idiosyncratic experiences rather than by the leading of the Holy Spirit.

An understanding of cognition can be helpful in our search for answers to biblical and theological disputes within the Church and between the Church and other communities. Theories of cognitive development can also be informative for other ministries of the Church.

Specifically, research in cognitive processes has proven useful for Christian Education. Jean Piaget and others have found that children think differently at different stages of cognitive development (Phillips, 1981). As infants they learn by connecting what they see, hear, feel, etc. with their own actions (the sensori-motor stage). Later, during the pre-school period, children learn through their own perceptions of the objective world (the pre-operational stage). During later childhood, thought processes become less bound to subjective perceptions (concrete operational stage). It is not until early adolescence that young people can use abstract reasoning (formal operational stage) as they seek to understand themselves and their world.

As a result of this modern understanding of how children learn, most Sunday school materials use age-appropriate methods in order to teach the timeless lessons of scripture. Pre-school students learn specific Bible stories. As they mature cognitively, school-age children learn more generalized lessons and by adolescence they are able to apply abstract religious concepts to their own lives, their world and their future.

Both in the counseling session and in the Sunday school room, cognitive therapy has made a significant contribution to the ministry of the Church. The concepts described in this chapter are not difficult to apply and the therapy has been shown to be effective, particularly in dealing with depression as well as anxiety.

Questions to Consider

1) What is the cognitive triad?

2) What is a schema?

3) Give four examples of cognitive distortions.

4) Give three examples of specific techniques of cognitive therapy.

5) Write a fictitious counseling session with at least 20 lines of dialogue that illustrate cognitive distortions. Include an analysis of that dialogue.

REFERENCES

Beck, A. (1963). Thinking and depression: Idiosyncratic content and cognitive disorders. *Archives of General Psychiatry. (9)* 324-333.

Ellis, A. (1973). *Humanistic psychotherapy: The rational-emotive approach.* New York: Julian Press.

............*Holy Bible: International Version* (1984). East Brunswick, NJ: International Bible Society.

Phillips, J. (*1981*). *Piaget's theory: A primer.* San Francisco: W. H. Freeman and Co.

Seligman, M. (1975). *Helplessness: On depression, development and death.* San Francisco: W. H. Freeman.

SUGGESTED READING

Beck, A., Rush, A. Shaw, B. & Emery, G. (1979). *Cognitive therapy of depression.* New York: Guilford Press.

Freeman, A., Simon, K., Beutler, L. & Arkowitz, H. (eds.) (1989). *Comprehensive handbook of cognitive therapy.* New York: Plenum Press.

Mann, J. (1973). *Time-limited psychotherapy.* Cambridge, MA.: Harvard University Press.

Persons, J. (1988). *Cognitive therapy in practice: A counseling session formulation approach.* New York: Norton.

Scott, J., Williams, J. & Beck, A. (eds.) (1989). *Cognitive therapy in clinical practice: An illustrative counseling session book.* London: Routledge.

CHAPTER VI
Marriage Counseling

When working with a married couple or a couple who are soon to be married, all of the previously described theories and techniques can be used. But marriage counseling requires a very different mind-set. When working with a couple, the goal is not an individual's well-being or personal growth. With a couple the primary concern is the marriage. The counselee is no longer an individual, nor are there two counselees - there is only one. It is the marriage that is the counselee.

The movement from individual to marriage counseling may be difficult for the inexperienced Christian counselor to make. The tendency is to attend to the two individuals who constitute a marriage rather than to the interaction between them. But in marriage counseling, the focus must no longer be intra-personal but interpersonal.

In addition, when working with a couple, the whole approach changes from a linear cause-and-effect understanding of a particular issue to a more organismic or holistic understanding. This important difference between individual and couple counseling requires further explanation.

When working with an individual counselee, the counselor seeks to ascertain what is the presenting problem. Sometimes the counselor will interpret the psychogenesis (*i.e.,* psychological origins) of that problem. Some counselors will focus on the treatment of the specific problem that the counselee wants to correct. Usually, the "cure" (and sometimes the cause) will be directly related to a specific problem. One might imagine drawing a straight line from cause to problem to cure. This is a linear mode of thinking.

When dealing with a relational issue, however, the linear approach is much less effective. Each spouse may have his or her own issues or problems that require some attention, but most of the couple's problems may only be present in the context of the marital relationship. That is, there is something about the dynamics between the two individuals that is more powerful than the specific issues of each.

Spousal abuse provides an excellent example of this concept. Most men who physically abuse their wives are not physically abusive outside of their own homes. But if, for example, the husband regularly abuses alcohol and also experiences too much stress, then he may strike out at his wife. Of course, most men who experience stress, even those who also abuse alcohol don't abuse their wives. Is the wife the relevant factor that makes the difference?

Maybe the wife adds to her husband's stress. She visits with her friends instead of cleaning their home and fixing healthy meals. She buys his liquor in large quantities and justifies her purchases by insisting that she is simply being "a good wife" by getting what her husband wants. Both husband and wife contribute to their dysfunctional relationship and each for his/her own (often unconscious) reasons.

Many people will find it highly objectionable to believe that the battered wife makes either a conscious or an unconscious contribution to her own abuse. Their objections are based on linear thinking. They see a cause (husband's uncontrolled anger) and an effect (battered and bruised wife). But the reality is that both husband and wife contribute to the husband's abusive behavior. This explanation does not excuse the abusive husband and certainly does not blame the wife for being abused. The husband is an adult who has to control his behavior regardless of the situation, just as the wife must control her behavior. It does, however, require that the counselor who works with such a couple - or any couple, focus on the interactions that take place in the marital relationship rather focus exclusively on the issues of each individual.

To focus on the marital relationship, however, does not mean that both spouses have to engage in counseling together. If only one spouse deals with the marital relationship, then the relationship can improve.[25] When one person in a marriage changes, the marital relationship changes and as a result the other person also changes. Marriage counseling is possible with just one person but it is usually better if both spouses engage in marriage counseling together.

Dealing with a relationship rather than with an individual is a difficult shift in emphasis for many counselors. Another difficulty in working with married couples is a very practical one. All too often, married couples fail to seek counseling until one of the spouses has already decided that he or she wants a divorce. It is not uncommon for a spouse to visit a lawyer first and a counselor afterward. If it is the wife who wants a divorce, for example, she may want a counselor to take care of her husband's emotional needs while the husband just wants the counselor to "fix" the marriage. Obviously the counselor cannot attend to these polar opposite goals.

If it is determined that the marriage cannot be saved, then the counselor may decide to minister to one spouse and recommend another counselor to minister to the other one. Individual counseling will probably include dealing with the grief that inevitably comes with the end of a way of life, the death of a relationship and the death of the hopes and dreams that the couple had shared. The empathic counselor will acknowledge the person's grief and deal with it the same way the death of a loved one is dealt with - the counselee will be encouraged to talk about his or her loss. Then, when the counselee is ready, the counselor will help the person look to the future. Perhaps the most important thing that the Christian counselor can do, is to help the counselee move toward forgiveness of both the counselee and the former spouse. (How to

---

[25] When an individual talks about a marital issue, he or she is speaking from his or her own perspective. But the attentive counselor can wonder out loud how the spouse would see the issue.

do this will be described in Chapter VIII).

Fortunately, many couples come for marriage counseling when the marriage is still relatively functional. They recognize that there are problems but remain committed to each other and to their marriage. Working with this kind of couple can be extremely rewarding. Two people who love each other provide a "holding environment." That is, they provide a warm and accepting atmosphere that allows each one to recognize and then change the attitudes and behaviors that are interfering with a fulfilling relationship. In comparison to individual counseling, couples are able to make amazing progress toward their mutually desired goals.

Regardless of the couple's degree of commitment to the marriage, there are a few issues that deserve special attention because they are so commonly experienced by married couples. These are; (1) failure in communicating, (2) triangles, (3) problems related to intimacy, (4) dysfunctional power arrangements and (5) sex. Each of these will be addressed briefly. Later, several fictitious counseling sessions will illustrate these issues and how to deal with them.

Probably the most common issue that couples want to address is their failure to communicate effectively. Communication involves talking and hearing. But it is more complicated than this description might suggest. Talking is more than mere spoken words. It includes the emotional tone of the words and the body language of the speaker. The same words can suggest very different meanings depending on how they are spoken. A simple phrase such as "are we going out for dinner" can convey a simple question, or a command to hurry up, or an accusation of incompetence that dinner has not already been prepared or a complaint about having to go out. These different messages are all enhanced with certain physical stances or behaviors. The speaker may stand with arms folded, may roll his eyes or lower his shoulders. These too convey certain emotional connotations. The speaker may not be aware of his body language but the person who is spoken to probably will be.

The words and behaviors of the speaker are then interpreted by the hearer. The interpretation may focus on the speaker's emotional tone and/or his body language. The interpretation may also depend on the kind of day the hearer has had or even the tone of voice that her father used with her. The impediments to effective communication are legion and many marriage counselors (as well as many counselees) believe that improving communications between spouses should be the focus of marriage counseling.

Some couples stop speaking to each other in any meaningful way because it is just too hard to even try. A husband stops talking to his wife because she never lets him finish his thought. The husband doesn't want to hurt his wife by criticizing her for interrupting him so he just stops talking. Or a wife stops talking to her husband because he wants to solve her problems instead of being emotionally attentive. He has no idea why she never talks to him but he doesn't even ask her why. The result is, they stop trying to really communicate with each other.

While it is true that when couples don't really talk to each other they can avoid painful arguments, it is also true that they lose any sense of intimacy with each other. That feeling of closeness, of intimacy, is difficult to achieve for some couples even when both spouses would like to have a closer relationship. But they just can't agree about how to achieve it.

People define closeness in different ways. Many men believe that closeness or intimacy means sex, while many women believe that intimacy means talking about feelings and their relationship. Both men and women often define intimacy as physical touching. All three activities constitute intimacy and healthy couples desire all three. When each spouse honors the other's understanding of intimacy, they are each more likely to achieve his or her own unique kind of closeness. The counselor would serve some couples well by simply asking each spouse how he or she defines intimacy.

Intimacy is a healthy and desirable feeling but too much intimacy can be a dangerous thing. The couples that find their soul mates in each other have discovered a wonderful relationship. The danger is that the soul mates can become intertwined with each other so that each loses a sense of his or her own individuality, his or her own uniqueness.

The healthy marriage allows for both intimacy and distance.

Couples enjoy being together; sexually, emotionally and physically but they also allow for each to pursue his/her own friends and interests. This healthy movement from intimacy to distance and back again can be difficult to attain if one person regularly requires more intimacy and the other wants more distance. Each believes that his or her need is "normal" and resents it when the spouse fails to meet that need.

The counselor who works with a couple whose needs for intimacy and distance are in conflict might point out these different needs and the value in each. Intimacy is a normal and valued part of the marital relationship - and so is distance. A satisfying relationship requires movement from one to the other. This back and forth between intimacy and distance in a healthy marriage takes place within a range that meets the needs of both spouses most of the time. A committed couple is likely to accept that their needs will not always be compatible.

Couples who find it difficult to navigate through changes in intimacy and distance find their own unhealthy ways to meet their needs. The most common way is to find someone or something else to meet their needs. The third party then becomes part of a triangle that includes husband, wife and other.

Sometimes triangles in the marital relationship are formed outside of the awareness of the couple. For example, when a couple has their first child, that newborn and the mother are appropriately enmeshed for the first few weeks of the child's life. Mother is empathically attuned to the baby's needs and enjoys the intimacy of the relationship as she meets those needs. Father often feels left out of that dyad.It is very easy for mother and child to keep father out of the system, especially since there is a mutual reciprocity of need gratification between mother and newborn. If father is comfortable with an on-going distance from his wife, then the triangle of mother, baby and father will persist. The baby has come between husband and wife just as powerfully as if one of the spouses had an affair.

If father is not comfortable with on-going distance from his wife, then he may find his own third party and form his own triangle. The third party may be a mistress or it could be his job. He may dedicate himself to his work where he finds emotional intimacy with a co-worker or the satisfaction that comes with accomplishment, respect and success. Just as the mother justifies her relationship with a newborn who does legitimately require her undivided attention and efforts, the father justifies his long hours at work as his obligation to provide for his growing family.

The potential for the formation of triangles in a marriage is almost without limit. The third party in a marriage could be in-laws, could be friends, sports and even church activities. When a couple seeks to avoid the back and forth of intimacy and distance (or any problem) they may turn to something outside the marriage on which to focus their time and attention.

Difficulties in communication, failure to negotiate the intimacy/distance continuum and triangles are three issues that plague marriages. The fourth frequently encountered issue has to do with the hierarchical structure of any relationship. In a marriage that structure becomes dysfunctional when one partner consistently exercises more control, more power than the other. Unlike communications, intimacy/distance and triangles, an imbalance of power is usually only a problem for one of the spouses, the one without power. The spouse with power will often not recognize that there is a problem and will typically be very resistant to changing his or her power position.

Every couple works out their power arrangements in subtle and unique ways. Some couples will resolve power struggles by tacitly agreeing that one spouse will have overt power and the other will have covert power. For example, the wife might seem to make all of the decisions about their shared life (overt power) while the husband feigns agreement but does whatever he wants to do (covert power). The problem with this kind of arrangement is that they never know how to establish and/or achieve goals that are desired by both of them.

Other couples will simply divide tasks and decisions according to cultural expectations. He does the outside chores and she does the inside ones. When it comes to making decisions, they will rely on the established "rules" of social expectations. When buying a car, for example, the husband chooses the model and the wife decides on what color the car will be. As long as power sharing is mutually satisfactory, then the couple has managed one of the potential problems that plague many marriages. But not all couples are able to share power in a way that is satisfactory to both spouses.

The counselor who works with a couple that has not been able to share power will usually focus on the spouse with less power. The reason for this is simple, the person with all the power has what she wants so has little incentive to change. If it is the husband who allows his wife to control his life and their relationship, then it is he who must reclaim his own legitimate power in relation to his wife. In addition, when the counselor focuses attention on the husband it enhances the husband's power for two reasons. First, the wife will hear, probably for the first time, that her husband feels powerless and second, some of the authority of the counselor is transferred to the husband by the counselor's attention to him. A note of caution may be in order here. The counselor who *takes the side* of the spouse with less power will find himself in the position of referee. That situation should be avoided at all costs. But paying more attention to one of the spouses is very different from taking sides.

For many couples, talking about power relations is difficult. But talking about sex is even harder. Some couples find it difficult to discuss their sexual needs with each other, let alone with a counselor. Yet a good sexual relationship can overcome many of the everyday struggles that any couple will experience. The Christian counselor should not avoid talking about this intimate subject if the couple is amenable to doing so.

One of the most common complaints relating to a couple's sex life has to do with frequency. When a couple disagrees about how often to have sex, it is usually the husband who wants it more often than his wife. He may complain that his wife is "never in the mood." The wife is likely to counter that criticism with her complaint that there is no romance in their marriage so she doesn't feel sexy. These common complaints can be dealt with in an honest and helpful way. Husbands can be encouraged to take their wives out on a date once in a while, and wives can be encouraged to think of themselves more as sexual beings who are at least willing to be aroused even when they may not be in the mood (Masters, Johnson, Grayson, Kolodny, 1986).

Sometimes the frequency of sex is related to the quality of the couple's sexual encounters. Sexologists have recommended that sexual partners should never let sex become routine (*ibid*). Within the comfort zone of both partners there should be new positions and varying tempos during sex. They also suggest that occasional sexual dysfunction should not be taken too seriously. There are many reasons for the husband or the wife to fail to reach orgasm and these are often only temporary. Worrying about these "failures" only adds to the couple's stress and leads to further problems.

Except for sex, the issues that have been presented in this chapter are not only applicable to married couples but to engaged couples as well (and some of them may also want to talk about sex). But counseling with couples who are engaged requires that counselors be aware of some of the roadblocks that may affect both them and their counselees.

One of the difficult parts of pre-marital counseling is that the couple may feel that they need to pass some kind of test. This is especially true when the pastor, rabbi or priest who will conduct the wedding ceremony is the pre-marital counselor. Couples are often afraid that the counselor will tell them that they are not well-suited for each other, or that they are too young or too old, their fears are real and numerous. These concerns can be addressed openly in order to ameliorate the couple's fears and establish a trusting relationship with the counselor.

An even more powerful roadblock to effective pre-marital counseling is the couple's idealization of each other. One of the elements of romantic love is that those who experience that emotion are loath to see any significant fault in the one who is loved. The couple who is in love is full of optimism and confidence and anything that might threaten that is very difficult for them to hear - and sometimes difficult for the counselor to say. These difficulties decrease, however, when the couple and the counselor are able to form a therapeutic alliance in which the hard realities of married life can be realistically confronted.

One effective tool in pre-marital counseling is the use of the genogram. A genogram is similar to a family tree. It is a family history, usually going back at least two generations, which shows how different members of the family related to each other. The assumption is that specific types of relationships are passed down from generation to generation so that the engaged couple will eventually repeat those relationships.

For example, a genogram might highlight the fact that the bride's mother and grandmother assumed more than their share of responsibility for the family, and as a result treated their husbands like irresponsible children. The husbands may have resented being treated like children but chose the path of least resistance and never told their wives about how they felt. This interaction between husbands and wives over the generations indicates that the bride may relate to her husband more like a mother than a wife. If the groom's father and grandfather were distant and uncommunicative, then the groom would probably not tell his bride that he was uncomfortable with her parental attitude toward him.

The counselor who uses a genogram simply points out the family patterns that are likely to be repeated by the couple. Once they are aware of these patterns, they are better equipped to recognize the problems when or if they happen. For further information on the genogram and how to use it, the reader is encouraged to consult *Genograms and Family Assessment,* (McGoldrick and Gerson, 1984).

The following fictitious counseling sessions will illustrate each of the previously described issues faced by most couples.

Fictitious Counseling Session I: Communication

Phillip and Hannah are in their early seventies. Hannah is well groomed and energetic, Phillip is slightly disheveled and unhealthy looking. The couple has been married for 51 years. They chose to sit on a couch side by side but they seldom looked at each other during the session. This is their second meeting with the counselor.

Line 1. Counselor: So, how are things going?
Line 2. Hannah: Well, I guess things are all right. What do you think (*turning to Phillip*)? (*Long pause*).

Line 3. Hannah *(to counselor)*: You see, he ignores me, I ask him a question and he refuses to talk to me. I just don't know what to do, I'm sick of being ignored.

Line 4. Counselor *(to Phillip):* Are you ignoring Hannah?

Line 5. Phillip: Well…

Line 6. Hannah *(angrily)*: Why don't you answer her?

Line 7. Counselor *(to Hannah):* Let's give him a chance to put his thoughts into words. Phillip?

Line 8. Phillip: Well, what was the question?

Line 9. Hannah *(angrily):* I asked you how you thought things are going at home. Do you think things are better or not?

Line 10. Phillip: I don't know *(long pause)*.

Line 11. Hannah: I don't know why I bother. I know you're tired, you work very hard, I know that. But we need the money, I do what I can *(to counselor)* we had to replace the roof and then we had to buy a new furnace. Now we're up to our ears in debt - I just don't know what to do *(long pause)*.

Line 12. Hannah *(to counselor)*: You see what I have to put up with? I feel like I'm all alone. Everything falls on my shoulders and he just sits there, he doesn't care *(crying)*.

Line 13. Counselor: I have a feeling that Phillip would like to respond to you but can't. You see, men's and women's brains are actually quite different. Almost from birth, women's brains work in such a way that we are able process language much more quickly than most men can. I can understand your frustration when Phillip doesn't respond to you but let's try something. I'm going to ask Phillip a question and neither one of us *(indicating Hannah and herself)* will say anything until Phillip has finished what he wants to say. Is that okay with both of you? *(Both nod in agreement)*.

Line 14. Counselor: Phillip, are you worried about your finances? *(Very long pause as Hannah fidgets with discomfort and Phillip opens his mouth to say something and then apparently changes his mind before he actually speaks)*.

Line 15. Phillip: I'm really putting in long hours but…

Line 16. Hannah *(interrupting)*: I know you are, I didn't say you weren't. I just…

Line 17. Counselor *(interrupting)*: Excuse me Hannah, but let's give Phillip a chance to finish his thought. *(To Phillip)* you were saying that you were putting in long hours?

Line 18. Phillip: I'm doing the best I can. I know that we have bills to pay, but I've got two jobs in the works, I'm pretty sure I can get some people who owe me money to at least give me something to pay down the bill. *(To Hannah, patting her knee)* we'll be okay.

Analysis

Line 1. The counselor does not assume that the topic that the couple spoke about in the previous session is the one they want to pursue in this one. So she starts with an open-ended question.

Line 2. When Hannah asks Phillip what he thinks, she may be acknowledging that she had pretty much dominated the first session and wants Phillip to be more engaged. But Phillip does not respond to Hannah in her time frame.

Line 3. Hannah is understandably annoyed with her husband and interprets his failure to respond as him ignoring her.

Line 4. The counselor asks Phillip if Hannah's interpretation is correct.

Line 5. Phillip begins to answer, but once again he seems unable to express himself within a time frame that fits Hannah's.

Line 6. Hannah seems to take some satisfaction in the fact that Phillip "ignores" the counselor as much as he "ignores" her.

Lines 7 - 10. Hannah's frustration with Phillip becomes even more evident and he reacts by saying even less.

Lines 11 - 12. Hannah expresses her anger at Phillip by going back to an issue that has plagued the couple for years - money. She is actually angry with him for "ignoring" her but chooses not to make herself vulnerable by exposing her hurt feelings so she expounds on another topic. This is a mistake made by many couples. They avoid feelings by bringing up past issues over and over again. But her anger and frustration are too much for Hannah and she cries.

The counselor does not respond to Hannah's tears for two reasons. First, she has already decided that the specific goal for this session is the couple's inability to talk to and listen to each other. Also, the counselor is reluctant to deal with the emotional concerns of one person rather than the dysfunctional communication of the couple. Once Phillip feels that he can express himself, it is he who appropriately attends to Hannah's feelings (line 18).

Line 13. The first sentence of the counselor's response is appropriate. Unfortunately she ends up giving the couple a lecture. Why? The information about the differences between the language abilities of men and women may be helpful in re-interpreting Hannah's feeling ignored by Phillip. But the lecture is much too long, indicating that there is something else going on here. The counselor shares Hannah's frustration with Phillip but is also angry with Hannah. The counselor sees Phillip as a hen-pecked husband and Hannah as the hen that does the pecking. So the counselor avoids expressing her own anger at both of them by becoming very intellectual and sounds more like a psychology professor than a counselor.

When the counselor makes the suggestion that Hannah give Phillip a chance to say what he wants to say, their response is significant. Neither one says a word. They feel the counselor's anger and simply nod in agreement.

Lines 14. The counselor asks Phillip about finances. She could have repeated the earlier question and asked how things are going, but this is too open-ended. For Phillip, talking about something specific and concrete may be easier than having to state an opinion.

Line 15. Phillip does not respond to the counselor's question. Instead he makes a plea to Hannah, he seems to be asking her to be less critical of him as a provider - he's doing the best he can.

Line 16. Hannah tries hard to obey the counselor's request (heard as a command) to let Phillip speak but it is obviously very difficult for her.

Line 17. Now the counselor does exactly what Hannah has been doing - she interrupts.In doing so she has unfortunately joined the couple in their dysfunctional communication. When there are powerful emotional undercurrents, as there often are with couples, the counselor is easily drawn into them.

[143]

Line 18. Phillip is given a chance to speak, possibly emboldened by the counselor's interruption of Mabel. He takes full advantage of his new sense of empowerment and responds to Hannah's concern about money. More importantly, he responds non-verbally to her feelings of rejection and loneliness by patting her on her knee.

During the first session the counselor made a quick assessment of the couple's commitment to each other as well as their capacity for insight. She decided that it would be best to focus on specific goals and to be very direct, even confrontational with them. This couple was determined to work out their problems and was not going to divorce because of them.

As to the counselor herself, she surely made some mistakes. She defended against her own anger by lecturing the couple and she engaged in the same dysfunctional behavior (interrupting) that needed to change. Nevertheless, the couple seems to have benefited from the counseling experience, as indicated by Phillip's loving gesture.

When a counselor feels angry, the best thing to do is to acknowledge that feeling to herself/himself and say as little as possible until the feeling has dissipated. If the anger has been expressed so that the couple is affected (as in this counseling session) then the counselor may ask the couple's forgiveness and explain his/her anger. In asking for forgiveness, the counselor maintains a sense of his/her own authenticity, which is important to both the counselor and the therapeutic process. With this couple, however, that would have been an unnecessary distraction from the task at hand so the counselor must simply accept the fact that her lecture was inappropriate and learn from the experience.

The counselor could also have interpreted her interruption of Hannah as an example of exactly what happens between the couple. But the interruption seemed to give Phillip the motivation to say what was on his mind. If the counselor had pointed out her own continuation of the couple's problem it would have taken the focus away from the couple, something that should be avoided if possible.

As for Phillip and Hanna, it could be that his slowness to speak may have been his way to avoid arguments with his wife. It seems that he would rather be the target of her anger than give vent to his own. Hannah took his non-responses as rejection of herself, which only fueled her anger at him. Once that destructive cycle was interrupted, even briefly, the couple was able to relate to each other in ways that permitted very real, if subtle, expressions of love.

Fictitious Counseling Session II:
Intimacy/Distance and Triangles

Jeff and Alicia are in their early fifties, they have been married for twenty-seven years and have one daughter who was recently married. Jeff is the pastor of a small church, Alicia works part-time in a local grocery store. The counselor, Helen, is Alicia's friend. She does not attend Jeff's church. The counseling session takes place on the telephone.

Line 1. Helen: Hello?
Line 2. Alicia: Hi, Helen. It's Alicia.
Line 3. Helen: Oh, hi, Alicia. How are you?
Line 4. Alicia: Well, not so good, that's why I'm calling. Do you have a few minutes?
Line 5. Helen: Yes, of course. What's the matter?
Line 6. Alicia: It's Jeff. He says he wants a divorce.
Line 7. Helen: A divorce? Alicia, what happened?
Line 8. Alicia: He says he's unhappy and has been for years. I just don't know what to do.
Line 9. Helen: Oh, I'm so sorry. (*Pause*).
Line 10. Alicia: I've been unhappy too, ever since our daughter got married. She and I were so close and when she left I thought I just couldn't stand it. You know, Jeff is always so busy with the church, people call him day and night and he works hard at being there for everyone who needs him. But he's never had time for me.
Line 11. Helen: So while Jeff dedicated himself to the church, you dedicated yourself to your daughter?
Line 12. Alicia: Well, yea. I guess that's what happened. We've grown so far apart I don't know if there's any hope for us anymore.

Line 13. Helen: Have you talked to Jeff?

Line 14. Alicia: No, not really. I just don't know what to say to him.

Line 15. Helen: Well, maybe you should tell him what you just told me. That you have each dedicated yourself to everything but your marriage.

Line 16. Alicia: Yes. You're right. Jeff and I used to talk to each other all the time, I mean really talk. Now's the time to pick up where we left off so many years ago. Thank you for listening, Helen. I don't know what I'd do without you.

Line 17. Helen: I will certainly keep you and Jeff in my prayers. I hope you know that I'm here for you any time.

Line 18. Alicia: I know, and thank you for your prayers.

Analysis

Perhaps the most unusual thing about this counseling session is that the conversation takes place on the telephone. The non-professional Christian counselor is likely to engage in counseling outside of an office, even on the telephone. The fact that Jeff was not included in the counseling does not mean that it wasn't marital counseling. The topic was the marriage, even though only one person spoke for the couple.

Alicia seems to be well aware of the problems in her marriage. She initially blamed Jeff for neglecting the marriage but also recognized that her dedication to her daughter was just as detrimental. Jeff's third party to the marriage was the church and Alicia had her own third party - their daughter.

Alicia could have ended up with two triangles. She spoke with her friend, Helen but not with her husband. Fortunately, Helen recognized the potential for being a third party in the marriage and advised Alicia to talk to Jeff directly. If Helen had offered to speak to Jeff herself, then she too would have become a third party. The couple was already dealing with at least two triangles, they didn't need to deal with another one.

Alicia and Jeff once had a healthy marriage that included emotional intimacy (line 16). But Jeff got caught up in his work with the church and Alicia got caught up with their daughter. The result of these two triangles was a growing distance between the spouses which neither one knew how to change. They may have been so involved with extra-marital activities that they were unaware of the ever-increasing distance between them - until Alicia's triangle broke. Her daughter left her.

Yet it was Jeff who wanted a divorce, not Alicia. It is possible that once Alicia no longer had her daughter as a friend and confidant, she tried to make up for her loss by drawing nearer to Jeff. His reaction was to create more distance by getting a divorce. He would rather maintain his distance and keep his mistress (the church) than change a relationship that over the years had become comfortable for him. Like individuals, couples are also resistant to change, perhaps even more so.

Alicia's decision to talk to Jeff was a good one for several reasons. First, she did not put Helen in the middle of her marital relationship. Second, she decided on her own solution so she was invested in it. Third, by acknowledging that she is part of the problem she opens the door for Jeff to do the same. Last and perhaps most importantly, talking about the problem is a form of intimacy that is highly beneficial to both Alicia and Jeff. Once the problem (triangles) is acknowledged by both partners, the solution (appropriate intimacy and distance) can be worked out.

Fictitious Counseling Session III: Power

After Alicia spoke to Jeff about the triangles in their marriage, the marriage improved for several months. Then they had a real shouting match, something that very rarely happened, so they decided to go to a professional pastoral counselor at a nearby pastoral counseling center. Alicia called to make the appointment and they were assigned to a pastor from a denomination other than their own.

Line 1. Counselor: So, what brings you here?
Line 2. Alicia: Well, a few months ago Jeff decided that he wanted a divorce. We talked about some of the troubles in our

marriage and things were really good for a while. But last week we argued and we both said some things that were pretty nasty.

Line 3. Counselor: Yes…

Line 4. Alicia: I'll admit that he earns more than I do, but I'm sick and tired of being treated like a child. He doles out money like it's all his and he's doing me a favor by giving me money for groceries and gas and a few little extras. Then he flies off the handle because I complain about it. I'm tired of his bullying!

Line 5. Counselor: Jeff?

Line 6. Alicia: Oh, he knows I'm right. He can't deny that he has complete control of the money and everything else. I just can't take it any more.

Line 7. Counselor *(to Jeff)*: Sounds like you're the boss and Alicia isn't very happy with that.

Line 8. Jeff: I guess. *(Long pause)*.

Line 9. Alicia: Well, that's not good enough. *(To Jeff)* I want to know what you're going to do about it.

Line 10. Counselor *(to Jeff):* Are you the boss? *(Long pause)*.

Line 11. Counselor: You know, Jeff. I'm getting the impression that you're not the boss. Alicia's been doing most of the talking, you're just pretty much agreeing with what she says. Are you the boss?

Line 12. Jeff *(angrily):* No, I'm not the boss. Yea, it's true that I take care of the finances, but when I walk in the door at home I know who's the boss and it certainly ain't me. 'Take off your shoes, don't sit on that chair I just upholstered it, I thought I told you to hang up your coat when you come in, why do I always have to pick up after you'? It never ends.

Line 13. Alicia: You know how the parsonage committee is. They think they can just drop in anytime and inspect the place. I can just hear them telling the whole church what a lousy housekeeper I am.

Line 14. Jeff: It's not just the house. You decide when and where we take a vacation, you decide what movie we go to. You decide everything.

Line 15. Alicia: Because you never decide. If it were up to you we'd never go anywhere.

Line 16. Counselor *(to Jeff):* So Alicia makes all the decisions because you don't and Alicia takes charge of what goes on at home because she's afraid of the parsonage committee. Who are you afraid of?

Line 17. Jeff: I'm afraid of her. She's so bossy all the time. She makes me so mad I'm afraid I'm going to really lose my temper so I just don't say anything. I just let her tell me what to do and I do it.

Line 18. Counselor: Alicia's afraid of the parsonage committee and Jeff's afraid of Alicia.

Line 19. Alicia: I'm sorry, Jeff. I didn't realize that I had become so bossy. I'm really sorry.

Line 20. Jeff: No, I'm sorry. I should have said something to you a long time ago.

Line 21. Counselor: Do you each accept the other's apology? Are you ready to forgive? *(Both nod their heads).*

Analysis

Line 1. The counselor addresses her question to the couple. She avoids asking how she might help them and in doing so puts the responsibility for change on Jeff and Alicia.

Line 2. It is not unusual for the wife to speak first, but that in combination with the fact that it was Alicia who made the appointment may suggest that counseling was more her idea than Jeff's. This can be interpreted as an indication that Alicia believes that she is the one without power.

Lines 3 - 4. The counselor waits in hopes that the couple will respond more fully. And it is Alicia who speaks again. She is very clear about her feelings. She describes Jeff as the one in charge, the one with all the power.

Line 5. The counselor forms a tentative hypothesis that it is actually Alicia who exercises control in the marriage so she directs her question to the one who may have less power - Jeff.

Line 6. The fact that Alicia responds to a question that was specifically directed to Jeff helps to confirm the counselor's initial guess. When Alicia presumes to read Jeff's mind ("he knows I'm right") the counselor is more convinced that while Jeff seems to have the power (he controls the money) it is Alicia who actually rules the roost.

Line 7. Again, the counselor addresses the question to Jeff, joining with him intentionally in order to share her power with him.

Lines 8 - 9. This is a typical exchange between two people when one person exercises overt power over the other. This imbalance of power requires that the powerless one is complicit, and Jeff fits this requirement.

Lines 10 - 11. The counselor joins Jeff and also confronts him.

Line 12. Jeff may be angry because of the counselor's confrontation. He finds it much easier to be angry with the counselor than he does with Alicia. But Jeff's anger may have also been the impetus for him to finally tell Alicia what he is thinking, that she is the one with power.

Line 13. Alicia is defensive. Jeff's outbreak of honesty takes her by surprise. So she diverts attention from herself and blames the parsonage committee for her behavior.

Line 14. Jeff is not going to let her off the hook. He complains about the unilateral power she exercises in other realms of their life.

Line 15. Alicia blames Jeff for the imbalance of power.

Lines 16 - 17. The counselor summarizes the marital dynamics and then takes a big chance. She challenges Jeff to say what has kept him powerless. The counselor assumed that Jeff was strong enough to tell Alicia how he feels. His newfound power is fueled partly by his anger and partly from being allied with the (powerful) counselor. This couple loves each other and seems committed to their marriage. So they are able to be honest with each other once the issue is out on the table.

Line 18. The counselor goes beyond the power struggle to suggest the cause - fear. This invites both Jeff and Alicia to take responsibility for their own behavior and to forgive each other.

Lines 19 - 21. The counselor makes a point of forgiveness. When a couple leaves a counselor's office they are sometimes much less polite with each other than they were in the presence of a stranger By stressing the grace of forgiveness, the counselor reminds them of their Christian faith and reduces the probability that they will engage in fruitless argument on the way home.

The life of a pastor and his/her family can be difficult. Parishioners can make unreasonable demands on the pastor's time, parsonage committees can be very intimidating and pastor's wives are sometimes treated like mere appendages of their husbands rather than as individuals with interests and activities of their own.

These special stressors are complicated by the fact that pastors find it hard to be helped - they are more comfortable as helpers. The problem is confounded by the need for an appropriate boundary between pastor and the church. (This issue will be explained in Chapter VIII). A church member may seek counseling from the pastor, but it would not be appropriate for the pastor to seek counseling from a parishioner.

In addition, the pastor often does not have a pastor. In some denominations superintendents, regional ministers or bishops may be pastors to the pastor but their services are fraught with problems. The pastor to the pastors is also the one who has input about the pastor's professional life. Because of the denominational hierarchy, it would be difficult for a pastor to tell his/her boss that there are marital problems. For these reasons, the professional pastoral counselor is especially suited to work with clergy and their families.

Fictitious Counseling Session IV: Sex

Byron and Cathy have been married for seven years. They have two children ages four years and one year. The counselor is their physician.

Line 1. Byron: Hi, doc. How are you?

Line 2. Counselor: Pretty good. How about you?

Line 3. Cathy: Hi, doc. We're both doing well, but we'd like to talk to you about something.

Line 4. Counselor: Okay, what's up?

Line 5. *(Byron nods to Cathy)*. Cathy: Well, we've been fighting a lot, and that's really not like us. We're fighting about money, about the kids, about our in-laws. Our marriage is not what it used to be.

Line 6. Counselor: Yes? *(Long pause)*.

Line 7. Cathy: That kind of stuff never really got our marriage off track before, but lately, our sex life isn't so good either. He just doesn't understand that when I get home from work I'm tired. I'm not in the mood.

Line 8. Byron: You're never in the mood. I know you're tired, but it seems like every time I come near you, you move away. I can't even give you a hug anymore.

Line 9. Cathy: Because every time you give me a hug I know that it's just the prelude to something else. And when it does become something else, well, it might be good for you but it isn't good for me. Slam bam thank you ma'am just doesn't do it for me.

Line 10. Byron: No Cathy. That's not fair. I try to meet your needs but you're not very helpful.

Line 11. Counselor: Okay, I get the message. Sounds like you've got a problem here. You probably know that it's not an uncommon problem, but that doesn't solve it, does it? So, Cathy is saying that she's not in the mood, partly because she's tired but also because her sexual needs aren't being met. Byron is saying that he wants sex more often and hasn't figured out a way to meet Cathy's needs. Right so far? *(They both nod in agreement)*. Byron, let me start with you. What do you do to help Cathy get in the mood?

Line 12. Byron: Well, I, uhm, I…

Line 13. Cathy: Right. You don't do anything to help me feel like a woman, like I'm sexy.

Line 14. Byron: You're right, hon. I'm sorry. From now on, we're going to put a little romance back in our lives. You know I love you, but I need to show it in special ways a little more often. And I will.

Line 15. Counselor: But there is another issue here. When you do have sex, it's not so great for Cathy.

Line 16. Byron: I really don't rush through it like she says. But it's really hard to turn her on. I used to, but now, I don't know.

Line 17. Cathy: Actually Byron, you almost never turned me on. I faked it so that I wouldn't hurt your feelings. I'm sorry. I should have been more honest with you. Is there something wrong with me, doc?

Line 18. Counselor: I don't know. I could give you a complete exam, but let me ask you something first. What might turn you on? Where does it really feel good when Byron touches you there?

Line 19. Cathy: I really don't know.

Line 20. Counselor: Okay, let me make a suggestion. You two need to explore each other's bodies. Cathy, you need to find out what turns you on and tell Byron what works and what doesn't. Ditto for you Byron. Treat sex like a wonderful adventure of discovery that you can share with each other. You know, we are the only beings on earth that have sex face-to-face. Sex is more than a physical act, it's our way to make the person we love happy. It's God's gift to us, to share the glories of sexual gratification with someone you love. Use the gift and have a great time.

Analysis

The couple's sexual problems are not unusual and they may not even be a serious threat to their marriage. But this couple wants more than a relationship that is merely functional. They understand that a good sexual relationship is one way to make a marriage so much more than just functional. So, like most couples who experience sexual problems they go to their doctor who, in this case, is a committed Christian.

The counselor listens carefully to the couple as they list their problems (line 5), but he guesses that their complaints are symptoms of something else. So he waits for the couple to address what else is on their minds (line 6).

Cathy and Byron talk about their unhappiness with the frequency of sex as each one offers what he or she believes to be the problem. They are probably well aware that frequency is a common problem for couples because there are so many jokes about it. So they are more comfortable talking about that issue (lines 7 and 8). Then Cathy gets to what is, from her perspective, the basic problem (line 9) while Byron responds from his own perspective.

As any one who deals with a couple should do, the counselor addresses the problem between Byron and Cathy before addressing each one's contribution to the problem (line 11). He begins with the issue that seems more comfortable for the couple, the frequency of sex and asks Byron to come up with a solution. When he is unable to do so, Cathy tells him what she wants and he agrees.

Part of the reason for the sexual problems seems to be a failure of communication. Cathy has apparently never actually told Byron that she needs to be treated like a "real woman" (line 13). Their inability to talk to each other is also clear in line 17. Cathy faked her orgasms rather than tell Byron that he was not meeting her needs. This is not unusual. The Hite Report (Hite, 1981) notes that about 53% of the women who responded to their survey faked orgasms. But faking it is not only unsatisfying for the woman, it is denying her husband the opportunity to share his pleasure with her.

The physician is aware that there are sometimes physical reasons for sexual dysfunctions in both men and women so he proposes a medical examination. But he is intuitive enough to wonder if the problem is more psychological than physical. So the physician/counselor questions Cathy about how much she knows about her own body. Our culture does not encourage women to explore their own bodies, so many women are unaware of what feels good, what arouses them sexually.

The Christian counselor not only addresses the couple's problems, he brings their sexual relationship into the context of their spiritual life. His reference to God's gift is related to science (only human beings have face-to-face sex) and probably not objectionable even if the couple is not religious. Sharing our faith (as long as it doesn't include moral judgments) seems to be more acceptable when it is within the context of care and concern for the other.

This fictitious counseling session illustrates the importance of a good sexual relationship, not only for the joy that sex brings to a marriage but also because sexual problems are usually intertwined with all of the other issues described in this chapter. The session included the need for intimacy (both emotional and sexual) it included the need for effective communication, the problem of triangles (the effects of work, in-laws and children on the couple's relationship) and even a problem related to power, although it was not addressed directly in the counseling session.

Cathy gave Byron the power to either satisfy her sexual needs or not. She did that by faking her orgasms. In so doing, Cathy gave her husband the power to decide something that she had a right and obligation to decide for herself. Yet, it is clear (lines 10 and 16) that Byron didn't want that kind of power. He wanted to share power and responsibility with Cathy for their mutual satisfaction. As in most cases of an imbalance of power, it was the one without power (because she gave it away) who needs to change that imbalance. In this case, Cathy has to tell her husband how to gratify her sexual needs. That is, she must not only exercise appropriate power but also claim the responsibility that power brings with it.

Biblical and Theological Reflections

Marriage counselors usually use the techniques of several different psychological theories. Most of those theories have already been assessed from a theological and biblical perspective. So for this chapter, the theological and biblical reflections will focus on the specific dysfunctions that have been presented rather than the theories that inform marriage counseling.

The problems that are most frequently present in dysfunctional or unhappy marriages are; (1) failure in communication, (2) an inability to move from intimacy to distance and back again, (3) the triangles that often result from avoiding intimacy and/or distance, (4) an imbalance of power between the spouses and (5) sexual problems.

Many stories in the Hebrew Scriptures illustrate these marital problems. What is especially notable, however, is that most of these "dysfunctions" are not considered to be problems by the biblical characters that were affected by them or by the writers who recorded them.

The story of Rebekah, Isaac and Jacob illustrates this beautifully. Isaac wants to give his blessing to Esau who is the older of his twin sons. But Rebekah's favorite son is Jacob and she wants him to receive Isaac's blessing. So she tells Jacob to trick his father, who was nearly blind, and pretend that he was actually his twin brother, Esau. The trick worked, and Isaac usurped his father's blessing, which, by custom, should have been given to Esau. (See Genesis 27:5 - 33).

The issue in this story is the failure to communicate effectively. Rebekah lied to her husband, Isaac. She participated in tricking him into doing what she wanted him to do. Rebekah made no attempt to disclose her wish that Isaac should bless Jacob instead of Esau. And Isaac, as was the custom of the day, made no attempt to consult his wife on such an important matter. There was a major failure to communicate between husband and wife, but the story is treated as simply an explanation for the lineage of the nation of Israel. Dysfunctional communications between husband and wife are not seen as important enough to merit any comment.

This same situation is also true about triangles. Perhaps the most famous marital triangle was between Abraham, Sarah and Hagar (Genesis 16: 1- 2). Although Sarah and Abraham had been promised that Sarah would bear a son, they both lost faith in that promise. Eventually Sarah told Abraham to take Hagar and have "the promised son" by her. Sarah introduced the third person into her marriage and that triangle has had historical significance for over three thousand years as the descendents of Hagar (Arabs) and Sarah (Israel) continue to kill each other. But the triangle itself was not perceived to be a marital dysfunction by Abraham or Sarah or the writer of the Book of Genesis.

As for the marital issue of an imbalance of power, both the Hebrew Bible and the New Testament are very clear about the exercise of power between a husband and wife. The power belongs to the husband and the wife is to obey him, according to scripture (*e.g.*, Ephesians 5:22). Does the patriarchy of ancient cultures apply to twentieth century America? The Christian counselor must answer that question for himself/herself before dealing with couples that have a problem sharing power. If the counselor's beliefs are more biblical than contemporary, then he/she must tell the couple that he believes that only the husband should have power in the marriage.

The people who are written about in scripture were real live human beings so it is not surprising that sex is a part of their stories. There is a euphemistic description of sex between Ruth and Boaz ("she lay at his feet") in Ruth 3:14, and we can even read about Onan spilling his seed (Genesis 38:9). But the sexual practices of biblical characters have little if anything to do with the sexual problems of contemporary couples. Frequency of sex, meeting each other's sexual needs, claiming responsibility for one's own sexual gratification, these are not mentioned in the Bible.

As for the intimacy/distance continuum, we just don't know. The Bible does not seem to have any interest in it. Again, there seems to be a real disconnect between scripture and contemporary marriage counseling.

The conclusion can certainly (but erroneously) be drawn that most of the problems that contemporary marriage counseling tries to address are either unimportant or are probably not problems at all. Certainly that is what the Bible suggests - unless the biblical stories and injunctions are understood within their particular time, place and culture.

During biblical times men made decisions so there was little need for effective communication between husband and wife. Triangles were not considered dysfunctional and in fact the patriarchs and kings of Israel all had several wives and concubines. And there certainly was not a women's movement that demanded that wives share power with their husbands. Even sexual mores have changed dramatically since biblical times. We live in very different times, our culture is radically different from that of both the Hebrew Scriptures and the New Testament. Do the practices of those early societies apply today? Again, the Christian counselor must address that question. The answer is not only important to a counseling ministry, but to our understanding of the Holy Bible as well.

Questions to Consider

1) How does marriage counseling differ from individual counseling?

2) What are the five most prevalent issues in marriage counseling?

3) Write a brief (5 to 10 lines) conversation to illustrate each of the five issues described in this chapter. Include a line-by-line analysis.

4) What is your own view of divorce? What would you tell a couple who came to you for counseling about your views?

5) If married, do you and your spouse define intimacy the same way? If not, what are the differences?

6) How do you deal with the differences between biblically acceptable marriages and modern marriages? Explain.

REFERENCES

Hite, S. (1981). *The Hite report.* New York: Dell Publishing Co.

............*Holy Bible: International Version* (1984). East Brunswick, NJ: International Bible Society.

Masters, W., Johnson, V. Grayson, V. & Kolodny, R., (1986). *Masters and Johnson on sex and human loving,* Boston:Little Brown.

McGoldrick, M. & Gerson, R. (1985). *Genograms in family assessment.* New York: W W Norton.

SUGGESTED READING

Masters, W., Johnson, V., Grayson, V. & Kolodny, R., (1986). *Masters and Johnson on sex and human loving.* Boston: Little Brown.

McGoldrick, M. & Gerson, R., (1985). *Genograms in family assessment.* New York: W W Norton.

Minuchin, S. (1974). *Families and family therapies.* Cambridge, MA: Harvard Univ. Press.

Scharff, J. (1989). *Foundations of object relations family therapy.* Northvale, NJ:Jason Aronson.

Witvleiet, C., Ludwig, T. and Vander Laan, K. (2001). "Granting forgiveness or harboring grudges: Implications for emotions, physiology and health." *Psychological Science, 12,* 117 - 123.

CHAPTER VII
Family Counseling

In many respects, counseling with a family is much like counseling with a married couple. The same topics that were described in the previous chapter apply to families as well. First and foremost, the family as a whole is the counselee, not each individual. In addition, members of a family need to listen to each other and tell each other their needs and wants. The spouses/parents need to cherish their marital relationship in order to maintain a healthy movement between intimacy and distance and avoid triangles. And of course, the parent/child struggle for power must be continuously re-negotiated as children mature.

It is important to note, however, that the fact that marital counseling was presented before family counseling was no mere coincidence. At the heart of every healthy family is a healthy marriage. Husbands and wives set the emotional tone for the entire family. If they "communicate" by screaming at each other, the children will do the same. If the marital relationship is always distant, then all of the family members will be distant from each other. For this reason many family counselors will, after the initial meeting, work exclusively with the parents/spouses even when the presenting problem is a child's behavior.

But a family is so much more than a married couple with children added. With each new addition to the family, the complexity of the relationships grows exponentially. This makes counseling with families very challenging. Added to this challenge is the difficulty that family counselors have in even knowing what is or is not a family. Our understanding of who constitutes a family has changed radically over the generations. So the first thing we need to do is define the subject. What is a family?

The family can be defined as a group of people who share blood and/or legal bonds. The members of this group often live together or have lived together in the past. The elderly grandparent living alone, the young adult living in a college dormitory and the sibling who has not been seen or heard from in many years are all still members of a family. Individuals always take the familial relationships with them, if not physically then certainly emotionally.

The main focus of this chapter, however, will be on families who live together. Sometimes the people who live in the same household are nuclear families consisting of parents and their children. Sometimes people create blended families that include two parents, at least one of whom has a child from a previous marriage or relationship. Or a family could be one parent or legal guardian and one or more children. The many different types of families living together are challenging our views about what constitutes a family.

While there are many different types of families, for the sake of simplifying a very complex subject this chapter will deal primarily with the nuclear family. Even these kinds of family are each different and unique, but they all have some things in common.

First, every family has a purpose, or to put it more precisely, two purposes that are in opposition to each other. Every family also has a number of organizing principles, ways in which family members interact on a day-to-day basis. These organizing principles include (1) traditions, (2) rules (3) roles, (4) boundaries and (5) the use of power.Each of these concepts will be described in some detail.

There are two main purposes that impact the way a family functions. First, every family must provide a safe, secure and emotionally nurturing environment for all of its members. Such an environment brings the members together in a relatively close-knit group. In a healthy family there is a considerable (but varying) degree of group cohesion (Gurman and Messer, 1995). The second purpose of every family is to allow the members of the family their own uniqueness in order to develop and flourish as self-governing individuals *(ibid)*.

In well-functioning families there is a continuous tug and pull between the needs of the family as a group and the needs of each individual member of the group. Some families that desire family unity are likely to be a close and cohesive group. Other families value each member's individuality and are more likely to lean toward being more distant.

A close-knit family enjoys the feeling of safety and security that comes when all of the members of the family value the family as a unit. A family whose members are more distant will promote independence, autonomy and self-actualization for each of its members. There is a wide range in the closeness/distance continuum among healthy families. But the critical element for healthy families is their ability to move back and forth between closeness and distance (just like a married couple). Each type of family will find its own unique balance between the need for togetherness and the need for individualization.

The dysfunctional family is one in which the members are so close that there is constant bickering because they are continually interfering in each other's lives. Or, a dysfunctional family might be so distant that the need for feeling safe and secure that a healthy family provides is not met. In addition to either of these two extremes, dysfunctional families fail to adjust to the changing needs of family members for closeness and distance. The balance between these two functions is never stable. It must change according to specific circumstances and also the developmental needs of each of the family members.

These then, are the two opposing purposes of every family: To be a cohesive whole while at the same time allowing the "parts" of the whole to remain distinct and separate. In order to maintain a balance between these two purposes, the family must live by certain organizing principles.

One of those organizing principles is the observation of certain family traditions. These can be everyday traditions like each member of the family having his/her own specific place at the table. Having a meal together is a tradition that has also been an important part of family life for many generations. It is a ritual that families keep in order to promote cohesiveness while at the same time giving each individual member the opportunity to talk about his or her own unique experiences of the day.

Special days such as birthdays, Thanksgiving Day and family re-unions are also traditions that provide cohesion and stability for families. To be sure, some of these special days are fraught with irritation, frustration and even conflict. Yet, families continue to observe these celebratory occasions. Why? Because the need to provide the stability and security that is one of the functions of families is stronger than the need to avoid the disappointments and frustrations that are sometimes a part of family gatherings when people express their own individuality.

Perhaps the most frustrating traditions are those in which individual needs are intended to conflict with the needs of the family as a group. A good example of such a tradition is gift giving at Christmas or Hannukah. Most families observe one of these two traditions. The emphasis on these holidays is (especially for children) the individual - the gifts *I* want to receive. When individual members of the family are encouraged to think only of themselves, the function of the family as the preserver of individuality overwhelms the other requirement of the family - stability and cohesiveness.

Observing certain rituals is an important organizing principle of family life. Another organizing principle is the establishment of and adherence to rules. The function of rules is to take some of the stress out of family relationships and to maximize the effectiveness of the family-as-a-unit's general functioning.

Healthy families have rules. They may be about when children go to bed, about regular attendance at work and school, about when each has control over the TV, etc. Of course, specific rules can change. As children get older they go to bed later. Sometimes rules can be temporarily broken. For special programs, one member of the family may choose a program even though it is not his or her turn to do so. Other rules may be set in stone - children are not allowed to play with fire, for example.

Unhealthy families operate at either of the extremes regarding rules. One kind of family requires strict obedience to the rules in order to meet their need for family cohesion and stability. Another family ignores rules in their over-emphasis on individual autonomy. Both types of families may function fairly well until the balance between these two purposes of a family is severely upset either from within the family itself or from life events that happen to every family.

Another organizing principle for every family is the adoption of roles by each member of the family. In this context, playing a role does not mean to pretend to be someone else. In the life of the family, assuming a role means that each individual's interactions with the other family members is somewhat predictable. For example, the wife might be the cook and the husband will be the family chauffer. Or the husband might be the family entertainer and the wife will be the serious one who gets everyone to do his or her chores. Both roles are of equal value and together they serve a real purpose. They maintain family cohesion because each one knows what to expect from the other.

Like rules, these roles are flexible in healthy families. Sometimes husbands and wives will take over the other's role when he or she needs help. Roles provide structure but the individual needs of each family member require that the playing out of the roles be flexible.

Children will also be assigned and/or adopt roles in the family. One will be the leader, one might be the jokester, one child may be the helper and another the loner. In a healthy family these roles will be assigned and adopted according to the personal characteristics of each individual. The children, like their parents will also require a certain amount of flexibility in how these various roles are lived out.

The purpose of roles, then, is to provide the entire family with an expectation of how (within a broad range) each person will act in the context of the family. The more each family can reasonably expect a certain familiarity about how each person relates to other members of the family, the safer and more secure they feel. In healthy families, the individuality of each person is respected while at the same time the needs of the family are also met. (The function of roles in unhealthy families will be described shortly).

Another principle of healthy families is that there are

appropriate boundaries between individuals as each also participates in the life of the family. One of the most important functions of rules and roles is to establish boundaries. Rules about personal space and roles adopted by individual members of the family all serve to draw a line - a boundary between self and other(s).

In each family, individuals need their own space to develop and mature. These private spaces are surrounded by invisible boundaries. It is as if each member of the family builds a wall between himself or herself and the rest of the family. This metaphorical wall keeps other family members from intruding upon their private moments and/or private spaces. Husbands and wives respect each other's boundaries when they don't listen to each other's private telephone conversations, when each one uses his or her own tooth brush, etc. Children establish their own boundaries around their own room or their own toys or their own activities.

While the establishment of appropriate boundaries is important, it is just as important that these boundaries, these metaphorical walls, also have doors (metaphorically speaking). That is, boundaries must be porous. For example, during a frightening storm, young children will jump into bed with their parents even though they would normally not be allowed to do so. Older children will let their younger siblings play with their toys occasionally and *vice versa*. Rules and roles establish boundaries for the well-being of each individual member of the family, but those boundaries remain porous for the sake of family unity.

Boundaries separate individuals from the group, they also separate sub-groups within the family. These sub-groups are called subsystems, a word that connotes the dynamic interaction within and between the subsystems (Minuchin, 1974).

The two most important subsystems are the parents and their children. If members of the extended family are a part of the family's everyday life, then they form a third subsystem whether or not they actually live with the nuclear family. Sometimes natural subsystems form that include a parent and a child, as for example, when a father and son share a passion for the same baseball team. But these *ad hoc* subsystems do not erase the on-going need for the separation between parent and child subsystems.

Establishing distinct subsystems initially requires significant parental involvement in the child subsystem. The parents are (hopefully) responsible adults and their children have not yet reached that goal. So it is the parents who establish the rules by which the child subsystem operates. But as children develop they may increasingly participate in establishing their own rules for their subsystem.

When children grow to maturity, of course, the functioning of the subsystems changes. The life of most families includes the eventual leaving of each child from the parental home. While this may initially be experienced as loss, in time the family bonds are re-formed as parents and their adult children relate to each other as adults of equal status. When that is achieved, the subsystems become porous almost to the point of no longer existing.

In many families, what had been the child subsystem takes on the responsibility of caring for their parents so that the parent subsystem becomes more like the child subsystem and *vice versa*. The changing nature of the subsystems as children grow to adulthood is often a difficult transition for members of both subsystems to make. But the family that has been both stable and flexible in the past will make the transitions with greater ease than the family that has not.

Another important organizing principle that healthy families manage is the ever-changing exercise of power according to the developmental needs of the children. With infants and toddlers, parents may exercise appropriate power by physically removing children from potential danger. The toddler who wants to move too close to a hot stove or steep stairway may be warned verbally and then picked up in order to prevent the child from getting hurt. As children mature, parents rely more on verbal commands than on physical actions to keep them away from dangerous situations.

As children develop, the exercise of parental power must adjust to their growing need for autonomy. Parents of a school-age child can request compliance rather than demand obedience. "Please clean up your room before you watch TV" is a request that is likely to be granted because both child and parent know who's in charge.

But by requesting instead of telling a child, the parent is subtly giving the child the power to decide to comply or not and in doing so is adjusting to the child's growing capacity for autonomy and individuality. Of course, parents of an adolescent child will also need to adjust their exercise of appropriate power. Because teenagers tend to be so changeable, knowing how strict the parent needs to be depends on the individual child at any given point in time.

The child subsystem also has its own subtle power arrangements. Older children will usually exercise more power within the child subsystem than will younger children. The older child will probably exercise power the way he perceives his parents use their power. If the parents respect the individual needs of each child, then the child subsystem is more likely to do the same. But there will be times when a member of the child subsystem endangers the well-being of some or all of its members. Sometimes parents need to intervene. The boundaries between subsystems must remain porous when it comes to exercising appropriate power by the parents.

As noted previously, one of the organizing principles of every family is the adoption of roles by each member of the family. The husband may be the "recreation director" while the wife is the "chief cook and bottle washer," for example. Children may play the roles of serious oldest child or spoiled baby of the family. But in dysfunctional families these roles can be devastating for a particular individual even while they save the family-as-a-unit from potentially destructive instability.

For example, in an unhealthy family one child may be the "good" one and the other the "bad" one. One child is unconsciously designated the pride of the family while another is the family scapegoat - the one who is perceived to be the bearer of all of the dysfunctional behaviors of every other member of the family. The family is able to survive with a certain level of functionality because one person becomes the focus of the fears and anxieties of all of them.

In family counseling, the scapegoat is called the identified patient (Bowen, 1978). This role can be assigned to and accepted by any family member, even one of the parents. This is always done without conscious awareness on the part of any of the members of the family, including the identified patient himself/herself.

When a child is the identified patient she may assume this role in order to stabilize the marital relationship. She might hear her parents arguing and be afraid that, like many of her friends, her parents will divorce. So by being the problem child she "demands" that her parents focus their anger on her instead of each other. The result is that the parental subsystem is strengthened as they join forces in their focus on their daughter's problematic behavior. The child unconsciously sacrifices herself for the good of the family. Of course, her sacrifice benefits her as well because she needs to maintain the family's stability too.

Many family counselors have found that identified patients will even risk their own lives in order to maintain some kind of stability for the family. Some cases of anorexia nervosa can be attributed to the need of a young person to become ill, and therefore the focus of attention, in order to alleviate intolerable stress and anxiety in the rest of the family system (Minuchin, Rosman and Baker, 1978). Unfortunately, it is too easy for the inexperienced counselor to dismiss the identified patient as "just looking for attention." When the family system is seen as a whole rather than simply a collection of individual members, then the appropriate focus of counseling is the entire family (but primarily on the marriage), not just the attention-seeking identified patient.

So far the discussion of family systems has focused on intact nuclear families. But more recently, such a family is in the minority in our society. Families are more likely to consist of a single parent and child/ren, or a couple (either heterosexual or homosexual) who is not married with children or any number of other arrangements that are too numerous to list. As a general rule, these types of families can be treated the same way as the nuclear family.[26] There is, however, a type of family that requires special consideration - the blended family.

---

[26] Even among single-parent families, the relationship between the former spouses may need to be addressed. Just because parents don't live together does not mean that the problems between them don't continue to affect the children.

In a blended family, children are brought to live together who are not related to each other nor are they related to one of the adults who form the parental subsystem. This extremely complex family brings together parents with different parenting styles and children who sometimes live with the family of the custodial parent and at other times live with the non-custodial parent. To say that this is a family in constant flux is to put it mildly. In such a family, the stability that every family needs and tries to achieve is constantly undermined. The result is increased stress and anxiety.

Blended families in significant numbers are a relatively new phenomenon and are therefore not especially well understood by family counselors (or anyone else). But the ever-increasing experience with such families suggests some basic principles that may be helpful.

First, stepparents should always remember that they play a different role than parents. Second, as with every family the spousal subsystem is of great importance to the functioning of the whole family and this is even more important for blended families. Each of these principles requires further comment.

The essential obligation of both the parent and the stepparent is to treat each child with respect for who he/she is.The child needs to feel loved and cared for by all of the adults who play a significant role in his life. That certainly includes his stepparent. But the stepparent with whom a child lives is less influential than the child's parents. In practical terms, this means that the main decisions about parenting a child are established by the parents, not the stepparent. The stepparent should follow the parents' lead and be supportive of the parent to whom he/she is married.

While the role of the stepparent in relation to the children of blended families is important for the well-being of the children, it is the roles of husband and wife that set the emotional "temperature" for the entire family. If the marital subsystem is fraught with arguments over child rearing, then all of the members of the family will experience heightened anxiety. In any blended family there will be many reasons for discord and unhappiness. The one relationship that is most important for the optimal functioning of the entire family is the marriage.

This focus on the marriage may seem unfair. We live in a

society that, at least verbally, treasures the child and believes that children must come first. To focus on the adults may seem unfair, especially when children are required to live with step-brothers and step-sisters whom they do not know and an adult who is not their parent. To put this concern in perspective, we can turn to the stewardess on an airline who tells the passengers that, if the air bags are needed, adults should put on their own mask before helping others. If the adults do not save themselves, they will be unable to save any one else. If the marriage is not "safe," then the children will not be safe either.

Fictitious Counseling Sessions

There are many different theories and techniques used in family therapy. All of the theories that have been presented in previous chapters have been adapted for work with families. The problem with these well-established theories is that they were designed for work with individuals and take a linear, cause-effect perspective.

There has, however, been a dramatic increase in the number of therapies designed specifically for working with families. Generally speaking, many of these new theories fall into two categories, they are either (1) family-of-origin or (2) structural. Some of the basic principles of each of these two theoretical approaches were presented in this and the previous chapter.

Rather than try to present the theoretical differences between these two types of family therapy (family-of-origin and structural) it would be better to focus on a more practical difference between them - that is, the stance of the therapist. The counselor using the family-of-origin approach (in the counseling session to be presented it is Family Systems) is usually more passive and uses interpretation of family history as its most important technique. In comparison, counselors who use structural theories are more active, confrontational and goal directed. The reader is encouraged to determine which theoretical approach is more suited to his/her personality as well as the needs of the family/counselee to whom he/she is ministering.

Session I: Family Systems

Pearl and Keith have been married for 22 years, they have three children. Bradley is 13 years old, Betsy is 15 and Sheba is 19. Sheba lives in her own apartment and works as a waitress. She rarely visits the family and was not present for the first two sessions but she is present at this third one. The presenting problem was the fighting between Bradley and his mother. The first two sessions were used to draw a genogram, which is a family history that included the relational patterns of the previous two generations of Pearl's and Keith's families of origin.

Line 1. Counselor: I'd like to go over what we discovered about your family histories in the last two sessions. What really jumps out at me (*to Pearl*) is how passive both your mother and grandmother were and (*to Keith*) how domineering your father and grandfather were. Do you see yourselves repeating the same pattern?

Line 2. Pearl: Well, I think that Keith wears the pants in the family. *(To counselor)* do you think I'm passive?

Line 3. Counselor: Well guys, (*to the children*) what do you think?

Line 4. Betsy: Yeah, I think mom just kind of goes with the flow, she isn't bossy or anything.

Line 5. Bradley: She sure bosses me around.

Line 6. Pearl: I don't boss you around, if you'd just do what you're supposed to do there wouldn't be a problem.

Line 7. Bradley: Yeah, right.

Line 8. Counselor: So Brad, you disagree with Betsy, you think that mom is bossy.

Line 9. Sheba: Mom is bossy. She is really bossy with Brad but she tries to boss us all around. Brad's the only one who won't let her get away with it.

Line 10. Counselor: Keith, is Pearl bossy with you?

Line 11. Keith: You better hope not. But I'm not home much so I don't give her a chance. All I know is that when I get home there's always a huge fight going with Pearl and Brad. I'm sick of it. Something better change here because I can't take much more of this.

Line 12. Counselor *(to Keith):* I'm wondering about you and Pearl. Does Pearl relate to you the way her mother and grandmother related to their husbands?

Line 13. Keith: What do you mean?

Line 14. Counselor *(to Keith):* Is Pearl passive in relation to you?

Line 15. Pearl: Yea, I guess I am.

Line 16. Counselor: So how can you both change this inter-generational pattern?

Line 17. Bradley: They'll never change.

Analysis

Line 1. The counselor draws attention to one of this couple's prevalent generational patterns. He chooses this pattern to focus on because he believes that it is the one that is the most problematic for the couple. It is Bradley's behavior that draws attention to this particular issue as he seems to be continuing the family's relational pattern. That is, Brad wants to be the domineering male like his father, grandfather and great-grandfather. His older sisters would not tolerate that from him.

Line 2. Pearl re-phrases what the counselor said. She does not want to call her husband domineering so she puts an acceptable slant on it - he "wears the pants." The motivation for Pearl's re-phrasing may be to maintain a level of stability. She would rather continue the family dynamics that have passed from generation to generation than to improve the functioning of her own family. For her, change means a loss of stability. Even when the change will improve the way the family functions, the threat of instability is stronger than the hope for a more loving and peaceful family.

Line 3. The counselor turns to the children, expecting a more straightforward assessment. Children are often very much aware of their parents' marital relationship and are less inclined to gloss over problems between them than are the parents themselves. They can risk change because the identified patient (Brad) maintains stability.

Line 4. It is Betsy who agrees that mom is rather passive, but she says nothing about her father's domineering behaviors. This is an indication that Keith is domineering not only in relation to Pearl but in relation to the children as well. Betsy is not comfortable being critical of her father, but she subtly (and probably unknowingly) suggests that Keith is bossy by not responding more fully to the counselor's question (line 1).

Line 5. Bradley does not relate to his mother the same way Betsy does. Pearl's mother and grandmother may have been submissive to their husbands but not in relation to their children. So Pearl continues that dynamic of her family of origin. She seeks to exercise appropriate power over her son while she remains submissive to her husband.

In addition, the fights between Brad and his mother serve an important function for this nuclear family. By becoming the identified patient, Brad draws attention away from his parent's dysfunctional and fragile relationship in order to maintain the family's stability. (The marital issue becomes clear in line 11).

Lines 6 - 7. Pearl and Bradley disagree with each other. She may be passive in relation to Keith but not with Bradley.Pearl wants the sense of stability that comes from replicating the relationships of her family of origin while Brad seeks stability as the identified patient who wants to save his parent's marriage.

Line 8. The counselor addresses Bradley directly, separating him from Betsy. This is probably a mistake. It focuses on the identified patient instead of the marriage.

Line 9. Sheba joins forces with Bradley and against Betsy. The counselor ignores this split in the sibling subsystem as he concentrates on the marriage. (The split will be addressed in the next counseling session study).

Line 10. The counselor focuses on the marriage by asking Keith about Pearl's behavior in relation to him rather than Bradley's interactions with his mother.

Line 11. Keith makes clear what everyone already knows. That, like the generations before him, he is the dominant one in the family. As such, he is also the most outspoken - in this case about his unhappiness with his family. There is a not-so-veiled threat that he will leave the family if there is not a change. But he does not see that he is the one who might also need to change. By implication, it is

Pearl or Bradley or both who must change their behavior if he is to remain in the home.

Line 12. The focus is, once again, brought back to the marital relationship. This time the counselor is more direct about Pearl's passivity in relation to her husband, but the counselor is not yet ready to specifically address Keith's dominating behavior as part of the problem.

Line 13. Keith is beginning to understand that the counselor is suggesting that he may be part of the problem. He asks for clarification.

Line 14. The question relates directly to the couple. It does not name Pearl's passivity alone or Keith's domineering alone, it is a question directly related to the way the spouses interact with each other.

Line 15. Pearl answers quickly, taking full responsibility for the marital dynamics. She may be afraid that if she included Keith's contribution it would be upsetting to him and the family's stability would be too threatened.

Line 16. The emphasis in the counselor's statement is on "both." It also draws attention to the fact that both Keith and Pearl are re-enacting family patterns of which neither was aware until they did the genogram.

Line 17. Bradley's position is to maintain the family as a group. He is the identified patient who unconsciously takes on the role of the problem child in order to save the marriage. He insists that his parents will never change because he needs them to stay the same - even though the consequences for him are so hard to bear. He would rather continue to fight with his mother than risk too much change in the family system.

Session II: Family Structure

The same family meets with a different counselor, one who uses a more structural approach to family counseling. This is a verbatim account of the second fictitious session.

Line 1. Counselor: I really enjoyed meeting all of you last week. Have you done the homework I assigned? *(Pause).* Remember I asked each of you to write down what your own chores were so that there would be less fighting about them.

Line 2. Bradley: Well, I guess I never got around to doing that, I don't think anyone else did either. *(The other family members nod their heads in agreement).*

Line 3. Counselor: Well, you each get thirty lashes with a wet noodle. Seriously, we won't accomplish anything unless you do the homework. So, for next week you have the same assignment. *(Pause, counselor looks directly at each person).* So, okay, how has this week gone for all of you?

Line 4. Bradley: Nothing's changed, mom still yells. No matter what I do it's never good enough.

Line 5. Betsy: Well, if you wouldn't argue with her all the time then maybe she wouldn't fight with you so much.

Line 6. Sheba *(to Betsy):* You're such a goody-two-shoes. You're always taking mom's side. Why don't you just shut up!

Line 7. Counselor: So it's Bradley and Sheba against Betsy and it's Betsy and mom against Bradley and Sheba. Okay, Betsy, I want you to come and sit next to your brother and sister. Now dad can sit next to his wife and the three kids can sit next to each other. Yeah, I mean it. *(Betsy moves to her assigned place, there is a space between Keith and Pearl where Betsy had been but Keith does not move).*

Line 8. Bradley: This is weird.

Line 9. Counselor: Good. *(To the children)* Betsy belongs with Brad and Sheba and Brad and Sheba belong with Betsy. You break up the family like you have been and it only spells moocho problems for everyone. From now on, when you come here, that's the way I'd like you all to sit.

Line 10. Keith: Well, it's about time someone told those kids what to do. I don't know why they can't do that for their mother.

Line 11. Pearl: I don't know either. Maybe I'm not strict enough with them.

Line 12. Counselor: That's probably true. What prevents you from being stricter?

Line 13. Keith: She's just a wimp, that's all. She can never stand up for herself and the kids know it. They take advantage of her. Believe me, when I get home they know who's the boss.

Line 14. Counselor: Well, as long as we're playing musical chairs, I'd like to change places with you *(to Pearl)*. Yea, I mean it. You sit in my chair and I'll sit over here *(indicating a chair next to the children)*. *(Pause)* I'm not kidding. *(They change chairs)*. So, how does that feel?

Line 15. Pearl: Kind of strange. I feel like I'm the one in charge all of a sudden. I don't think I like this, but I think I could get used to it.

Analysis

Line 1. From the very beginning, the counselor establishes herself as the one in charge. She gave the family a task to be done at home and expected it to be completed.

Line 2. It is Bradley who speaks for the family. This can be taken as an indication that he sees himself as the one with the greatest investment in the family as a unit.

Line 3. The counselor insists that the family must follow her directions, but does so with humor. This is an intentional technique of structural therapy. It is meant to alleviate some of the stress that change in the family always causes. The counselor then turns over the control of the session to the family.

Line 4. Bradley speaks for the family again. He gives verbal proof that his need is to maintain the family's structure without change. He announces that what he wants has been accomplished, that the family has not changed. He goes on to draw attention to the presenting problem. He and his mother are maintaining the same troubled relationship.

Line 5. Betsy assumes her role as mom's ally.

Line 6. Sheba announces her position. She is allied with Brad and against Betsy.

Line 7. Alliances and alignments are an important part of structural family therapies. The counselor makes the alignments explicit and immediately moves to change them by having Betsy move away from her parents in order to join the sibling subsystem. But Keith does not follow the counselor's implied directions. He leaves the space open that Betsy had taken between her parents.

Keith is not going to be told what to do. The counselor's directions were not specifically to him because she sensed that he would not comply and didn't want to antagonize him too much. As in any therapy, the counselor needs to be accepted by the family if meaningful goal is to be accomplished.

Line 8. Bradley speaks for the sibling subsystem. The new seating arrangement is threatening because it changes the family's way of interacting with each other.

Line 9. The counselor says that it's good that the siblings are uncomfortable. Their discomfort indicates that they are aware that a significant change has taken place in how the family functions. She then goes on to explain, in every-day language, why she insisted on the new arrangement.

Line 10. Keith is well aware that his position of dominance has been usurped by the counselor. He decides to speak up and be heard. He makes it clear that the children and *their mother* are the problem. He has nothing to do with their dysfunctional interactions.

Line 11. Pearl has a need to "unruffle" Keith's feathers. She hears the anger in his voice and wants to establish a different emotional tone. She does that by assuming responsibility for the family's problems. This is probably her role in the family, to try to keep everything pleasant - except when it comes to Brad.

Line 12. The counselor confronts Pearl believing that she can stand up for herself.

Line 13. Keith intervenes. He is critical and demeaning of Pearl and states the obvious, that he's the one with most of the power in his family. He displays his power by pointing to Pearl's lack of power but does not seem to realize that he might be the reason for Pearl's lack of authority with the children. (The Family Systems counselor alluded to this imbalance of power by speaking of Pearl's passive and Keith's domineering ways of relating to each other).

Line 14. Again the counselor gives instructions, this time with a little bit of humor about musical chairs. She must be insistent with Pearl who is very reluctant to assume the "throne" - the position of power that the counselor's chair represents.

Line 15. Pearl's reaction to assuming this power-by-association is hopeful. She is uncomfortable with the newness of her position and all that it implies in relation to Keith as well as the children. But once she has tasted power she realizes that she has a right to it.

Comparative Analysis of the Two Sessions

One of the most significant differences between these two sessions is the emotional tone of the family. In the first counseling session, the family seemed considerably less anxious than in the second one in which the family's anxiety is reflected in an increase in the number and intensity of angry exchanges. The counselor who confronts a family is likely to increase their anxiety, which while uncomfortable, is also likely to result in change. The more uncomfortable a family is, the more they want to ameliorate their discomfort. "No pain, no gain."

The systemic approach relies more on understanding than emotional reactions so the counselor calmly and rationally points out that the family is re-playing the relationships of their own parents and grandparents. This approach assumes that the family's current unhappiness is enough of a motivation for the family to make the necessary changes.

Another difference between the two theories of family therapy has to do with what topics the counselor believes to be the most important. For example, in Systems Theory the sibling subsystem is given very little attention nor are the dysfunctional alignments between the sibling and marital subsystems. In structural family counseling the dynamics of the previous generations are only relevant in as much as they might relate to current family functioning, and even then are considered tangential.

The different approaches also require two very different types of interactions between the counselor and the family. In the first counseling session (Systems Theory), the counselor was primarily interested in interpretation of the genesis and the continuation of dysfunctional family dynamics. It was left to the family members themselves to decide if they wanted to change those dynamics. The structural approach was much more confrontational. Homework was assigned and the counselor expected it to be done. She was far more interested in changing the family than simply helping them to understand themselves and each other better.

[179]

The counselor who is more comfortable with helping counselees understand their problems than actually participating in changing the family will probably be drawn to the systems approach to family counseling. For the counselor who wants to actually accomplish change, the structural approach may be more appealing.

The counselor who is familiar with both theories and comfortable as either one-who-enlightens or as an agent of change should pick and choose which family or situation is better served by which theory or combination of theoretical approaches. A highly dysfunctional family with poor insight and limited capacity for verbal expression would probably be better served by the structural approach to family counseling. A family given more to rational understanding than emotional outbreaks may benefit more from Systems Theory.

While the family systems and the structural approaches are very different, there are also important similarities in the two types theories. Specifically, both consider the marital relationship the key to family functioning and both recognize the necessity of working through the natural resistance to change that families (and individuals) have. And perhaps most importantly, they both focus on family interactions and relationships as opposed to treating each family member as an individual rather than as a member of a group.

Biblical and Theological Reflections

Family counseling, with its emphasis on functionality, raises a theological question related to the goal of all counseling. Specifically, should the goal of counseling be functionality or happiness? When psychologists and counselors think about families they do not search for ways to make people happy. Psychological theories are concerned about families being functional, which is not the same as being happy. But counselees come for help because they want to be happy not merely functional. They know that they are very unhappy and they don't like it. They are not interested in merely being able to handle what life throws at them. They want to overcome adversity, not just survive it. Psychological theories and the people who may benefit from them are at odds about the goal of therapy.

Sigmund Freud had his own views on the goal of therapy. His Psychoanalytic Theory is, like most theories, concerned with how people function in the world, not about their happiness. Yet, he was very critical of God's plan for humanity because it does not seem to include being happy. Freud recognized that "the common man" wants to be happy. If God is a loving God, argues Freud, then God should have established a world in which people could be happy (Freud, 1961). Of course, Freud ignores the biblical teaching that Adam and Eve were expelled from the Garden of Eden so they lost their best chance at happiness. Nevertheless, Freud is probably correct in his belief that most people do want to be happy.

Fortunately, the Christian counselor has a great deal more to offer than a mere feeling, which is all that happiness is. The Christian counselor can be a vessel of God's healing power as a first step toward relieving emotional suffering and then go on to offer the counselee the road to victorious living.

How are we to achieve this wondrous state, this attitude toward life? The way is both very simple and very challenging. "Love the Lord your God with all your heart, with all your soul and with all your mind. This is the first and greatest commandment. And the second is like it. Love your neighbor as yourself" (Matthew 22: 37-39).

We can either understand this commandment as implying that God is so needy that He commands us to love Him or that the commandment is more for our sakes than God's. The second alternative seems far more likely. Jesus tells us to love God, our neighbor and ourselves because that is the way that we will ever have a rich, fulfilling and meaningful life.

Counseling is a valuable first step in alleviating the suffering of individuals and dysfunctional families. But for the Christian counselor that's all it is - a first step. When suffering has been alleviated, then we can offer the great commandment as the essential element in a life that has the quality of eternal life. We invite the counselee to live out the gift that we have given to him or her or them.

Questions to Consider

1) Describe three attributes of well-functioning families.

2) Referring to the previous chapter as well as this one, describe three attributes of dysfunctional families.

3) How do triangles meet the needs of families? What are the potential disadvantages of triangles?

4) Which is the most important subsystem in all families? Discuss what makes this subsystem so important. What are the potential threats to this subsystem.

5) Compare Family Systems Theory with Structural Theory. Which theory appeals to you? Why?

6) What do you believe is the way to real joy?

REFERENCES

Friedman, E. (1985). *Generation to generation: family process in church and synagogue.* New York: Guilford Press.

Freud, S. (1961). *Civilization and Its Discontents,* J. Strachey, (trans.). New York: W.W. Norton,

..........*Holy Bible: New International Version* (1984). East Brunswick, NJ: International Bible Society.

Gurman, A, and Messer, S. (1995). *Essential psychotherapies: Theory and practice.* New York: Guilford Press.

Minuchin, S. (1974). *Families and family therapy.* Cambridge, MA: Harvard University Press.

Minuchin, S. Rosman, B. and Baker, L. (1978). *Psychosomatic families: Anorexia nervosa in context.* Cambridge, MA: Harvard Univ. Press.

SUGGESTED READING

Bowen, M. (1978). *Family therapy in clinical practice.* Northvale, NJ: Jason Aronson.

Minuchin, S. (1974). *Families and family therapy.* Cambridge, MA: Harvard University Press.

Minuchin, S. & Fishman, H. (1981). *Family therapy techniques.* Cambridge, MA: Harvard University Press.

CHAPTER VIII
Conflict Resolution

The Christian counselor's ministry need not be limited to individuals, couples and families. The Christian counselor may also be called upon to minister to an entire congregation, especially one in conflict. So this chapter will apply counseling techniques to the life of a local church. First, the question of how to avoid turning an argument into a church-wide conflict will be addressed. Later, the techniques for resolving a conflict will be described.

There are four important ways to prevent an argument from turning into a conflict that affects an entire congregation. These are; (1) follow the rules, (2) use power appropriately, (3) avoid triangles and (5) understand and respect the differences between pastoral and lay leadership.

As is true of any group, there will always be disagreements in the church. The inevitability of disagreements comes from the fact that the group is a collection of individuals, most of whom have their own ideas about what a group (or other individuals in the group) should or should not do. Sometimes these disagreements are between a few people who just don't like each other and the problem remains between them. At other times disagreements affect the functioning and ministry of the entire church. These are the disagreements that every Christian must be able to address.

The good news is that if disagreements are dealt with effectively and in a timely manner they can be good for the group as well as the individuals who constitute the group. When people disagree it is because each member of the group is able to express his/her own individuality. When disagreements are resolved, individuals feel respected for their uniqueness and the group is strengthened in its cohesiveness as it gains confidence in its ability to function well when people disagree.

Unfortunately, some disagreements among members of a congregation or between a congregation and the pastor become conflicts. A conflict is very different from a disagreement. A conflict can be defined as a disagreement in which *emotions* prevent people from reaching a satisfactory solution to a disagreement.

For example, a member of the congregation (we'll call her Dora) doesn't like the organist's accompaniment of the congregational singing. She thinks that he plays too slowly. So she goes to the organist ("Stanley") and tells him exactly that. Stanley can then have one of two responses. He may tell Dora that he appreciates her input and will pick up the tempo on those hymns that warrant a faster tempo. The argument was settled by a compromise. Stanley will play at least some of the hymns faster and Dora's opinion has been validated. Both of the participants can consider the issue closed, it was a win-win solution because emotions did not get in the way.

Or, Stanley may consider Dora's suggestion to be an insult, he is hurt and responds angrily. His anger may be expressed directly to his critic or he may simply ignore Dora's suggestion and go on playing the congregational hymns as slowly as he has been. When Dora hears Stanley play the hymns, she also feels hurt and angry.

The tempo of the hymns is no longer the most important issue. Stanley believes that he has been insulted and he is angry. Dora believes that she has been ignored and she too is angry. Both parties have allowed their feelings to get in the way of resolving the problem. A disagreement has become a conflict.

As often happens in any group, the conflict does not stay between the two people involved. Stanley may complain to the pastor that people just don't appreciate him, "all they do is criticize." And Dora may tell her friends in the church that the organist should be fired because he is so smug and insulting. "He had the nerve to tell me to mind my own business." Both of these reports are interpretations of what was said or not said, and neither is objectively true. But each of the parties now has an ally. And these allies validate two very different "truths" for the two antagonists just by agreeing (or by not disagreeing) with each of them.

Inevitably the whole congregation is affected by the conflict. Some of the members will take Stanley's side and some will take Dora's side. Of course, most of the congregation will take neither side. Their involvement in the life of the church is rather peripheral, in part because they don't want to get embroiled in the inevitable squabbles that happen in any church. But even these members will experience the growing anger between the two factions in this conflict. They may not be involved in the conflict directly, but they are certainly affected by it.

A simple disagreement has become a church-wide conflict. One of the reasons that the dispute between the organist and the parishioner escalated into a conflict is that neither one followed the rules. Dora should have taken her complaint about the organist to the appropriate committee; perhaps the worship committee, or the personnel committee or the church council. And Stanley should have asked that same committee if other people had complained about the tempo of the hymns.

To be sure, not every disagreement needs to be dealt with in such a formal manner but when there is a doubt about how two people might handle a difference of opinion, following the rules is always the best option.

The second reason that a disagreement between two people turned into a church-wide conflict was that there was a failure to exercise appropriate power. That is, the only people who have the authority to ask the organist to play the congregational hymns faster didn't use their authority to settle the disagreement. Of course, they couldn't act because they probably never even knew that there was a problem. If either Dora or Stanley had informed the appropriate committee about their disagreement, then that committee could have taken appropriate action. The argument could still end in a win-win situation *if* the chairperson of the committee who speaks to each of the antagonists is blessed with the capacity to express the committee's decision in a caring and effective manner. (More about that shortly.)

Assuming that the members of each church committee are either elected or appointed to serve on that committee, they have the authority and the obligation to resolve contentious issues. In order to meet that obligation, the committee must exercise their power. When every one knows who's in charge of a particular endeavor in the church, power struggles can be kept to a minimum. When there are struggles over power it is often because one person or committee has abdicated their position of authority and another person has assumed it.

But power must always be exercised with sensitivity. The person with the authority that has been granted by election or appointment has power. That person can "lord it over" others or be more egalitarian. He or she can be either authoritarian or authoritative. The authoritarian leader will issue an order and demand that it be obeyed. The authoritative leader can talk to people like adults and find a solution that does not result in anger, jealousy and an on-going struggle for power.

Related to power struggles is the third major cause of conflict within the church (or any organization), which is the formation of triangles.

One of the common failings of pastors as leaders of a congregation is to allow themselves to be caught in a triangle between two disputing parties. For example, when Stanley came to the pastor to complain, the pastor should have directed him to the appropriate committee in order to ask them if they thought he was playing the hymns too slowly. When the pastor allowed herself to get in the middle of the conflict the organist could justifiably assume that the pastor was on his side. The pastor may not have been on Stanley's side at all; she may have simply listened to him without commenting. But in any conflict, perceptions are usually more important than objective realities (Bridges, 1991).

Unfortunately, the organist-pastor-parishioner triangle was not the only one. When Dora complained to her friends she created another triangle, the one that consisted of herself, her friends and the organist. Creating triangles in a church is a real danger to the entire church. The tragedy of forming these triangles is that disagreements can never be resolved. Two people have to actually talk to each other (not a third party) in order to resolve their disagreements.

The fourth reason that arguments become conflicts is that the leaders of the church, lay and/or clergy, have failed in their obligation to lead. In any group, including a church, the leader is the most important person for the optimal functioning of that group. Churches have one leader (the pastor) but lay leaders also assume responsibilities which require them to exercise their authority.

The leader of the religious life of the church is the pastor. Those in charge of the temporal life of the church are usually the lay leaders. Many conflicts arise when the leaders of these two separate and distinct realms usurp the authority of the other. Let us consider these two types of leaders separately and then see how they interact as they carry out the church's mission.

The pastor is the leader of the congregation to which he/she has been called. Like every leader, the pastor must have some connection with the members of the group. The leader who is not involved with the members of the group is not likely to have any followers because most people want to know their leader. They are far more likely to follow someone they know than a stranger. They want to have some kind of personal connection with the leader if they are to follow him or her.

Effective pastoral leadership, then, means that the pastor and the parishioners share a mutual sense of connection to each other. In the course of his/her ministry, the pastor will certainly nurture that connection. The pastor will participate in people's lives in a unique way as parishioners share with him/her their most intimate secrets. When the pastor buries a loved one or conducts the marriage ceremony for members of the church that pastor participates (in a very special way) in the lives of the people involved.

Every pastoral leader, then, must participate in the life of the group. But every leader must also be separate and distinct from the group. People want to know that their leader is different in some way from the members of the group. If the leader is not more qualified or more experienced or more knowledgeable, then why shouldn't the group simply follow someone else- one of them, for example?

What makes the pastor separate and distinct from the congregation is his/her calling by God and ordination by a denomination or congregation. Church members are willing to follow the pastor because he or she has been authorized and therefore empowered to lead. It is the pastor's ordination and/or calling that makes him or her different from all of the members of the church.

So every pastor must be separate and distinct from the church while at the same time be involved (sometimes intimately) in the lives of the members of the church. This dual role is problematic. Effective pastoral leadership requires managing this delicate balance between being the minister who serves and the leader who leads. (The reader who is interested in how to maintain the balance between these two roles is referred to Friedman's book *Generation to Generation*).

As important as pastoral leadership is, lay leadership also plays an essential role in the life of the church. The laity governs the practical life of the church. They know about maintaining the church building and grounds, they know about book-keeping, insurance, office equipment, contracts with plumbers, electricians, they know someone who will cut the grass, etc. The ministry of the laity is just as real and important as the pastor's ministry.

This is not to suggest, however, that the church has more than one leader. The pastor is the leader of the congregation because the church is first and foremost a religious institution. When the laity assume a leadership role that usurps the authority of the pastor, then the church is no longer a church, it loses its identity, its very reason for being. It becomes a business instead of a church. When the pastor usurps the authority of the laity, he or she is inviting a struggle over power.

So clergy and lay leaders must each respect the domain of the other. The pastor is the religious leader and the laity are responsible for the practical issues that must be attended to for the optimal functioning of the church. There are times, however, when the practical life of the church cannot be separated from the religious life of the church. When that happens clergy and laity must work together to find a solution with which they can all agree. But more often than not disagreements between clergy and laity are not as practical as who's going to keep track of the church's finances or who's going to fix the office copier.

Sometimes personal issues are at the very heart of a problem. This is especially true when a disagreement is between the pastor and members of the congregation. Unfortunately, some lay leaders choose to ignore these kinds of issues - to sweep them under the rug.

Holding the pastor accountable for his/her behavior is difficult for most members of a congregation. People respect the office of the pastor; often the pastor is loved and appreciated by the members of the committee that is supposed to address issues that involve the pastor. But no pastor is perfect; there will always be legitimate complaints that must be addressed by the committee that is appointed by the congregation to hold the pastor accountable. When that committee ignores a problem that involves the pastor, the problem does not go away. It grows like a cancer and inevitably explodes into a conflict that would have just been a disagreement if it had been handled in a timely manner.

One reason for holding a pastor accountable is that the church needs a leader whom the followers can respect. The lay leaders must also be held accountable, for the same reason. Both lay and clergy leadership are essential to the functioning and ministry of the church. Both must be held accountable for the good of the entire church.

These then, are the most common causes of conflicts in a church or any other group; people do not follow the established rules. There is a struggle over power because the leader who has authority fails to exercise his/her appropriate power. Sometimes triangles develop so that the entire congregation, including the pastor, becomes involved in a disagreement between two individuals. Sometimes both lay and pastoral leadership are compromised. The laity wants to avoid problems and in the process they create conflict. As for pastors, the balance between being a friend and minister to members of the church and also being the leader of the church has not been achieved.

Whatever the cause of conflict in the church, there are

important principles that can be applied in order to resolve those conflicts. These are; (1) listening to the other, (2) stating the problem clearly, (3) recognizing cognitive distortions, (4) valuing feelings, (5) being flexible and (6) being forgiving.

One of the most common mistakes that people make when they are in conflict with each other is that they don't really listen (Bolton, 1979). Listening is more than just hearing what is said, it involves hearing what is implied, what feelings are being expressed as well as being aware of how both the listener and the speaker are affected by those feelings.

As noted in a previous chapter, hearing what is said is more difficult than it may sound. Every listener has his/her own filter through which communication must pass. For example, a member of the building and grounds committee, we'll call him Bob, reports that the plumber did a poor job installing the new furnace. "Mitchell" is a plumber (not the one who installed the furnace) and hears Bob's statement as a criticism of his profession. So Mitchell responds "what makes you an expert on furnace installations"? The plumber wasn't listening to the problem; he only heard what affected him emotionally. He felt that he was being attacked and responded to his own feelings instead of the actual problem - the furnace was apparently not working well.

One reason that Mitchell did not respond to the actual problem was that Bob did not state the problem clearly. He should have simply said that the furnace didn't seem to be working well. His criticism of the plumber was meant to convey that message, but he did not address the problem directly so Mitchell misinterpreted it. When trying to resolve a conflict, stating the problem as clearly as possible is the first task. Once people can agree as to what the real problem is, then it is more likely to be addressed without hurt feelings (Bolton, 1979).

But even stating the problem clearly is fraught with difficulties because of cognitive distortions. For example, Bob assumed that a furnace that was installed properly should heat the whole building to the same temperature. The cognitive distortion was in treating his assumption as if it was a fact. Bob was convinced that if the whole building is not heated to the same degree, then it is because the furnace was not installed properly. But it may be that there are

[192]

more windows or there is less insulation on the cold side of the church.

The failure to make a distinction between assumption and fact often leads to another cognitive distortion. Specifically, "if my assumption is wrong then I am wrong." For some people, being wrong is the same as being bad; a failure, an idiot and therefore completely unacceptable as a human being. Pointing out this distortion is so difficult because by doing so, the person perceives that his distortion is a mistake, is wrong, and therefore all of the negative self-perceptions must be true.

When trying to resolve a conflict with a person who cannot admit to himself or anyone else that he may be wrong, the importance of being right to this person must be addressed. One might ask for example "what's so important about being right?" This has two advantages. First, it temporarily takes the focus away from the problem; the solution to which may not be possible when one person must always be right. Second, it allows the person to reflect on his own thinking and self-perception and possibly recognize that his thinking is distorted. There are times, however, when addressing this kind of distortion is best done in private in order to avoid embarrassing the person who must always be right.

The embarrassment of being wrong is not the only feeling that prevents the resolution of conflicts. When people are hurt they usually become angry. If they express that anger at the person who hurt them, then that person may express his/her own anger in return.

Venting feelings does not resolve conflicts. And contrary to common belief, it does not necessarily relieve the tension of the person who vents.[27] If anything, venting increases a person's anger and leads to feeling humiliated and guilty for losing control of one's emotions. When people express their anger inappropriately, their feelings must be acknowledged and then, if necessary, they may be given an opportunity to apologize. In any case, it is best to stop for a moment and ask everyone to take a deep breath before

---

[27] The concept of venting comes from Sigmund Freud's understanding of "psychic energy."But those who have studied this concept have never accepted it as valid. Unfortunately, it remains a popular idea.

the discussion continues.

Sometimes anger is expressed covertly, but that can be just as non-productive. A person may say, for example, "you know I say this in Christian love, but you're crazy for thinking that way." This is surely a double-edged sword. The speaker hides behind "Christian love" and hurls an insult that cannot be addressed because it is done in "love." When this happens, the speaker must be confronted for the good of the group. If it is not, then everyone who may disagree with the speaker will be afraid of his irrefutable attacks.

Fear of confrontation, concerns about losing control of one's emotions or being attacked by another are all very real impediments to resolving a conflict. It is primarily up to the leader to provide a safe environment for the group. This means keeping the expression of intense emotions to a minimum and allowing people to talk about their feelings without expressing them inappropriately. There is a big difference between telling the group "I am really feeling very angry right now" and shouting obscenities and/or insults.

Feeling angry, or any other emotion, is a normal human experience. It is how one expresses emotions that may have a negative effect on the group that is trying to resolve a conflict. If emotional outbursts cause fear and embarrassment, then it may be more productive to take some time off or to reframe the problem at hand (Fisher and Brown, 1988).

For example, if the conflict about how the furnace works evokes angry insults, then the issue might be reframed by asking if the windows in the cold part of the church need to be fixed, or if it would help to close the doors when the rooms are not in use. After tempers have cooled, then the group might address the furnace problem more directly.

Dealing with intense feelings requires that the process of conflict resolution be very flexible (Bridges, 1991). When conflict occurs, most people will want to resolve it quickly. Conflict is uncomfortable for the individuals involved, for the group that is trying to resolve the conflict and for the entire church. It is natural to want to do everything possible to alleviate the discomfort quickly. But sometimes fast is not best.

A common method of preventing conflicts from escalating is to table a contentious issue. The group simply decides not to deal with it at this time. If the church leadership takes the opportunity to deal with individuals separately in order to explore feelings and cognitive distortions, then tabling an issue could be a good tactic. If, however, the leadership or other members of the group use the temporary halt in order to lobby for their own position, then the conflict can only intensify.

The time to address the problem again should probably not be established at the meeting at which it was tabled. The more flexibility in timing, the more likely there is to be a positive outcome. Flexibility in the process of conflict resolution is at least as important as flexibility concerning the outcome. And flexibility regarding the outcome of a conflict is usually essential. That is, disagreements or conflicts often require a solution that is a compromise between competing views.

For many churches, however, the most difficult conflicts have to do with theological issues for which there may not be a compromise. But even these conflicts can be approached with flexibility.

One of the most difficult issues facing many denominations has to do with attitudes about gays and lesbians. Each side of the argument has valid scriptural and theological sources to support their view. Those who believe that gays and lesbians should not be allowed to join the church quote Leviticus 18:22 and from Romans 1:26, 27. Those who welcome gays and lesbians note that chapters seventeen and eighteen in the Book of Leviticus require that those who eat meat with blood in it are also guilty of grievous sin.How might the principle of flexibility be applied to this conflict?

First, the conversation between people who hold opposing views might also include people who are not normally included in congregational or denominational conflicts. For example, a congregation might invite a practicing homosexual and/or lesbian to address them. The congregation might also invite members of other churches that have already resolved the issue to come and speak to them. The church might provide a study group to learn more about homosexuality. Whatever the issue, it can always be addressed with flexibility even when a compromise is not possible.

Even the most difficult problems that churches face can

eventually be solved if certain principles are followed. And once the problem is solved, that must be the end of the matter. The issue must not be raised again. People whose suggestions were not followed, people who have an inordinate need to have their own way, people who believe that they were not heard may try to over-turn a decision. All that does is keep the conflict going. If a difficult issue is raised again, and especially if the original decision is rejected, no good outcome can be expected. Of course, if circumstances change, then the issue can be re-visited. Otherwise, once a decision is reached, everyone must respect it.

In the process of the development and resolution of conflict, people will almost inevitably hurt each other. Therefore, the most important principle of conflict resolution is forgiveness. If nothing else, the Church should be an expert at forgiveness but that is seldom the case. Churchgoers find it just as difficult to forgive people who have hurt them as anyone else does. Yet, we tell God every time we pray the Lord's Prayer that we do forgive our debtors or those who trespass against us. This chapter will conclude with some general comments about the art of forgiveness.

Jesus asked God to forgive the people who crucified Him because "they do not know what they are doing" (Luke 23:34).Many times during a conflict people say and do things that are hurtful. The people who are hurt would do well to ask themselves if the person who made a cutting remark, for example, did so knowingly. Did the person know what he or she was doing? When we remember how often we have unwittingly hurt someone, forgiving that insensitive person is as essential as forgiving ourselves.

It is also essential to recognize that the anger that increases when we fail to forgive is much more harmful to ourselves than the person who hurt us and therefore needs forgiveness. The physiological reaction to anger is high blood pressure, gastro-intestinal problems (including weight gain), sleeplessness, depression, anxiety, etc. The inability to forgive will make us physically ill and actually shorten our lives (Paloutzian and Park, 2005). A failure to forgive only prolongs and increases the effects of the hurt that requires forgiveness.

One of the most powerful roadblocks to forgiveness is for an individual to go over the conflict in his/her mind and tell other people over and over again about the people and events that hurt him/her. Reminding ourselves over and over again about the person who hurt us prevents us from forgiving that person and only increases our own pain. Repeating the hurtful event to others has the same effect and, in addition, sows discord in a congregation.

Being human means that when we have suffered at the hands of another, we find it very hard to forgive that person. Once we accept that our Christian faith requires that we forgive others, we find that forgiveness is seldom accomplished once and for all. When Peter asked Jesus how many times should he forgive his neighbor, Jesus told him "not seven times but seventy-seven times" (Matthew 18: 22). Whenever the person or event that hurt us comes to mind, we have to forgive all over again.

Another common roadblock to forgiveness is the mistaken idea that we are obligated to forgive a person if *and only if* that person apologizes. But this act of contrition may not be offered for any number of reasons.In such a case we must remember "while we were yet sinners, Christ died for us"If God did not require that we ask forgiveness for a list of specific ways in which we disobeyed God and hurt others, then who are we to require it?

In any conflict, both parties and factions will be required to forgive the other. This is especially true when the conflict is between a parishioner and a pastor because continuing such conflicts affect the entire church even more than a conflict among parishioners.

There are probably more conflicts between a pastor and parishioners in a church than there are among parishioners. At least part of the reason for this may be that parishioners have expectations of a pastor that they do not have of each other. Many churches have expectations that are, to say the least, very unrealistic. And sometimes members of the same church have conflicting expectations of what the pastor should do or even what kind of personality he or she should have.

Some people want the pastor to be outgoing and gregarious, others want the pastor to be serious and sensitive, still others believe that the pastor should be who he/she is - as long as it's exactly like (or exactly opposite of) the pastor they had before. The possibilities for conflict with a pastor are almost without limit.

In the following fictitious meetings, the pastor and the Pastor Parish Relations Committee (PPRC) meet in order to deal with some issues that have been brought to the committee's attention. The first meeting is a disaster. The second meeting, with the same fictitious people, demonstrates some of the concepts that have been presented in this and previous chapters.

Fictitious Meeting I

Tom is the chairman of the PPRC. Dick and Harry are members of that committee. They have asked the pastor to come to this meeting in order to address some concerns that have been reported by some unnamed parishioners.

Line 1. Tom, Dick and Harry: Hi, pastor. Come on in.

Line 2. Dick: We have some issues that we'd like to bring to your attention.

Line 3. Harry: Yea, a lot of people have been complaining about you.

Line 4. Pastor: What seems to be the problem?

Line 5. Dick: Well, I have several letters that I'd like to read.

Line 6. Pastor: I don't think…

Line 7. Dick: The first one says that you're not friendly. You never say hello to people, you just don't care about us. You're so distant and unreachable. We don't need a pastor who doesn't even like his parishioners.

Line 8. Pastor: Well, I really don't know…

Line 9. Harry *(angrily):* I have a couple of letters too. One person thinks that you don't visit people who aren't coming to church. Our income has gone down since you've come and we need more people who will contribute.

Line 10. Pastor: Actually, that's not…

Line 11. Harry: My son feels the same way. We used to have two services on Sunday morning and now we only have one. I want to know why you cancelled the early service. Just because you can't get an organist for the first service doesn't mean we can't have one. You can certainly find someone who will come and play. A lot of people looked forward to coming to church early so that they could have the rest of the day to themselves. You know, people with families like to go out and do things together. For a lot of them Sunday is the only day they have to do that. I remember when the church used to be full, now we're lucky if we get 50 to 60 people. I think it's time for you to leave. It's either you or me.

Line 12. Tom *(shouting):* I feel the same way.

Line 13. Dick (*shouting*): We want your resignation right now or we're all leaving and a lot of people will be coming with us.

Analysis

A brief survey of the problems with this meeting should be sufficient. They are all too clear. First, the leader of the committee did not lead. He did not exercise the power that comes from his position as chairman. The result was a meeting that soon got out of control. Tom's failure to maintain any kind of order is especially evidenced by the inability of the pastor to get a word in edgewise.

Second, the PPR committee exceeded their authority. They are not allowed to ask for the pastor's resignation. The committee may suggest that course of action to the congregation but they cannot usurp the power of the congregation as a whole.

Third, when Dick and Harry read the letters, they introduced a third party into the problem - they created a triangle. The pastor, if he had been allowed to respond, might have satisfied the readers of the letters, but not the writers. When a triangle exists, there is no way to resolve the conflict.

In addition, the piling on of complaints was counter-productive. In any conflict it is essential to deal with a specific problem, not a litany of problems that were, in this case, unrelated to each other.

Finally, Harry (line 11) seemed to think that everything was the pastor's job. The pastor is responsible for the church's finances and the pastor should find an organist to play for an early service. Harry did not differentiate between the pastor as the religious leader of the church and the laity's leadership in the practical life of the church.

Not only did the committee do all the things that create conflict, they also ignored the basic concepts for resolving them. The first complaint attacked the pastor without stating a specific problem (line 7). None of those present gave the pastor a chance to speak so there was no way for them to listen to him (lines 4, 6, 8 and 10). There was no room for any flexibility in resolving the problem because the committee had already decided on the solution (line 13). There was an unstated assumption (a cognitive distortion) that it is the pastor's responsibility (and only his) to fill both the coffers and the pews (lines 9 and 11). None of the speakers showed any recognition about how the pastor might be feeling nor did the committee members seem to be aware that their own feelings were getting out of control.

Finally, the committee's solution was actually a lose-lose. If the pastor leaves because of the committee's threats, the church loses a pastor. But the church would more than lose their religious leader. The church's governance will continue to be unacceptable and even destructive.

If the pastor stays, the church not only loses some of its members, but the committee seems determined to split the church into pro- and anti-pastor. The committee is determined to implement the worst of all possible alternatives because they were so focused on their own inappropriate use of power that they failed to see that their obligation was to the entire church, not just themselves.

In the following verbatim, the same people were present and the same issues were brought up. But in this meeting, the five principles for resolving conflicts were followed. People listened to each other, the problem was stated clearly, the cognitive distortion was clarified, they each respected the feelings of everyone else and they were willing to be flexible in resolving the issues that were discussed. Perhaps the most important element in this meeting, however, is the willingness of each person to accept responsibility for his own behavior and to apologize (ask forgiveness) when that was required.

Line 1. Tom: Hi, pastor. Please come in and have a seat.

Line 2. Dick: Tom, I have something that I'd like to bring up.

Line 3. Tom: Okay, Dick. What's on your mind.

Line 4. Dick: Well I have a letter here that I'd like to read to you. My wife has several complaints about the pastor.

Line 5. Tom: I'm sorry to interrupt, Dick. But if your wife has complaints about the pastor, don't you think she should tell him about it face-to-face?

Line 6. Dick: Well, she says that she said hello to the pastor the other day and he ignored her.

Line 7. Tom: The by-laws of the church require that complaints about the pastor be made by the person who has them. So Dick, I'm afraid I'm going to have to cut you off. Can you see why it isn't fair to let you go on?

Line 8. Dick: Yeah, I guess you're right. And the rules are the rules. Can't live with 'em and can't live without 'em. *(They all laugh)*.

Line 9. Pastor: Tom, I wonder if I might speak to Dorothy's (Dick's wife) concern.

Line 10. Tom: Sure, go ahead, pastor.

Line 11. Pastor: I'm going to have to give Dorothy a call and apologize. Sometimes I get so caught up in my own thoughts that it's like I'm in a daze. I certainly didn't mean to ignore her but I can also understand why she felt hurt. I'll give her a call as soon as the meeting is over.

Line 12. Dick: You know, I have to tell you. I felt kinda bad about even bringing it up. I shouldn't have, I'm sorry pastor.

Line 13. Tom: Any other issues that anyone wants to talk to the pastor about?

Line 14. Harry: *(Angrily)*. Yes, I want to ask the pastor about what he does all day. We've got fewer and fewer people coming to church and less and less money to pay the bills. Don't you think that he ought to go and see people more, get them to come church?

Line 15. Pastor: Tom, I'd like to respond to that. *(Tom nods in agreement)*. I think that there are two separate issues here. First, what do I do all day. I thought you knew, Harry, that pastor's only work one hour a week *(they all laugh)*. But seriously, every day is different. If you'd like to know what I do all day, I'd be happy to start keeping track of my time and show you *(indicating all of them)* my schedule the next time we meet. Is that all right with everyone? *(They all nod in agreement)*.

As for the second issue you raise, that's a little more complicated. You seem to think that it's my job to get people to come to church so they can help pay the bills. Two things I'd like to say about that. First, it's everyone's Christian responsibility to invite people to come to church. In fact, studies show that people are much more likely to come to church when they're invited by a friend or neighbor than if the pastor invites them. As to getting more people to pay the bills, is that really what the church is all about? Do we care more about how much money we rake in than we do about the ministry of the church? I don't think any of us feel that way.

Line 16. Harry: Well, I still say we need more people in church.

Line 17. Pastor: Harry, maybe you and I can have a cup of coffee early next week and talk about that some more. I'll get my calendar and we'll see when we're both free. Is that okay with you?

Line 17: Harry: Sounds good.

Line 18. Tom: Well, if no one has anything else, we'll close this meeting. Pastor, will you lead us in prayer?

Analysis

Line 1. Tom alone welcomes the pastor. The other members respect his authority as the chairman of the committee and therefore the one who extends a welcome on the part of all of them.

Lines 2 - 4. Dick addresses the chairman for permission to speak. This allows Tom to be in charge of the meeting and to maintain appropriate rules of order. Dick then starts to read the letter from his wife.

Line 5. Tom didn't allow Dick to get too far into the letter. He explains why he interrupted and apologizes for doing so. Tom is well aware of the destructive nature of triangles - they prohibit a satisfactory conclusion because the person who is complaining is not there.

It should be noted, however, that when many people make the same complaint about the pastor (or the organist or any other individual) then the committee can speak for all of them. In that case the committee is empowered to speak for others.

After interrupting Dick and mildly rebuking him, Tom gives Dick an opportunity to correct his own mistake so that Dick can "save face." That is, Tom recognized that Dick might have felt embarrassed and tried to assuage that feeling.

Line 6. Dick doesn't listen to Tom. Instead, he continues to read the letter. But at least the problem was stated clearly rather than calling the pastor names ("unfriendly" and "uncaring") as in the previous verbatim.

Line 7. This time Tom is a little more authoritative. He uses both reason and the law to make his point. The leader of every committee must know the rules that govern the conduct of that committee. He cannot expect that everyone is going to do as he suggests, so being able to remind the members what the rules are is an unassailable reason for Dick to stop reading the letter.

Line 8. Dick is a little embarrassed by what he now acknowledges is his mistake. He then adds a little humor. In any meeting a little bit of humor can go a long way in relieving the tension that is bound to arise when people confront each other.

Lines 9 - 11. The pastor acknowledges that he is not the leader of this committee by asking Tom's permission to speak. When Tom gives him permission, the pastor explains his behavior. Most importantly, he acknowledges Dorothy's feelings and promises to apologize to her.

Line 12. The pastor's respect for Dorothy's feelings may have given Dick the opportunity to express his own, he felt bad about bringing up the issue. Like the pastor, he apologizes for his own behavior.

Line 13. Tom recognizes that the meeting is going well. Each man can voice his own concerns without undue worry about how his concerns might be received.

Line 14. Harry is angry. He doesn't direct his question to the pastor directly. He treats the pastor as if he isn't there. But Tom doesn't address Harry's anger. It may be that he understands that Harry is uncomfortable confronting the pastor and his discomfort comes out as anger. So the chairman doesn't turn the meeting into a counseling session. The confrontation has not yet turned into a conflict because the pastor does not respond angrily (next line). It takes two to turn a disagreement into a conflict.

Line 15. Now the pastor is on his own turf, the biblical and theological. Nevertheless, he correctly asks for permission to speak. The pastor avoids a conflict with Harry by being conciliatory - up to a point. He offers to share his schedule, not just with Harry but also with the entire committee. In doing so, he does not give to Harry alone the authority that rightly belongs to the entire committee. The pastor also inserts a little humor to assuage the tension that Harry's comments cause.

Then the pastor addresses the content of Harry's assumption (that it is only the pastor's job to get more people to church). He enhances his authority (perhaps defensively) by referring to a study. The pastor then becomes a teacher of scriptural principles, the church's ministry is not for the purpose of paying the bills.

Line 16. Harry only knows what he already believes and doesn't hear anything else. This is the cognitive distortion of selective abstraction. It is also a way to not lose an argument.

Line 17. The pastor doesn't want to end up with a win-lose solution. Instead, he offers to meet with Harry in a social setting. They'll meet for coffee instead of the pastor's office because the pastor does not want to exercise his authority (and the power that comes with it) in order to "win" the argument.

The suggestion that the issue be discussed one-to-one shows creative flexibility in the process of conflict resolution. The pastor may use the occasion to talk about Harry's cognitive distortion when they talk outside of the committee meeting.

Line 18. Tom acknowledges that the pastor is the religious leader of the church by asking him to lead them in prayer. Tom is the acknowledged leader in the temporal realm and the pastor is the acknowledged leader of the church as a church. There is no competition between the two of them.

Biblical and Theological Reflections

The Bible is replete with conflicts; some military, some political and some theological. For example, God's promise of a land flowing with milk and honey was realized only after many military battles with the inhabitants of the Promised Land. Saul and David were in a political conflict for years over who was the anointed king of Israel. And of course, much of the New Testament was written in order to address theological arguments having to do with the position of gentiles in the Church or disagreements regarding accepted practices of worship, etc.

The contemporary Church is no longer engaged in military conflict but conflicts over power and theology continue to abound. These conflicts can be resolved by using the principles that apply to resolving all conflicts. In the local congregation, however, conflicts are often between individuals who just plain do not like each other, they have what is commonly referred to as a personality conflict.

The Acts of the Apostles also records personality conflicts, some of which were never resolved. The individuals who had the conflict simply went their separate ways. The disagreement between Paul and Barnabas (Acts 15: 36-40) is a case in point. Barnabas wanted to include John, also called Mark on the missionary journey with Paul. But Paul disagreed so he didn't take either Barnabas or John, he took Silas instead.

Did Paul not take kindly to being told what to do by his disciple? Did Barnabas resent being treated like a subordinate? We can't be sure of the answers to these questions, but they suggest that Paul and Barnabas had a personality conflict. Fortunately, this clash of personalities did not result in a less effective ministry for Paul. God's power continued to manifest itself through him.

Similarly, not every conflict in the Church of today can be resolved. It is important to use every tool at our disposal to resolve conflicts, but sometimes they cannot be brought to a successful conclusion. When the conflict cannot be resolved because of personality conflicts, one or both of the parties involved will often leave the church. When that happens, those who leave should be respected and loved and encouraged to find a local congregation in which to worship and fellowship. Conflicts do not need to be seen as failures, they can also be seen as a new beginning for those who stay as well as for those who leave.

Questions to Consider

1) Describe the balance that every pastor must maintain between being a minister to individuals and the leader of the church.

2) Describe three techniques to use when resolving a conflict.

3) Do the people in your church know the rules of governance? If not, what can you do about that?

4) How are differences in biblical interpretations handled in your church? Could you use the techniques of conflict resolution to ameliorate those disagreements?

5) Do you believe that lay or clergy leaders are best suited to handle conflicts in your church?

REFERENCES

Bolton, R (1979). *People skills: How to assert yourself, listen to others and resolve conflicts.* New York: Simon and Schuster.

Bridges, W. (1991). *Managing transitions: Making the most of change.* Reading, MA: Addison Wesley Publishing.

Fisher, R. and Brown, S. (1988). *Getting together: Building relationships as we negotiate.* New York: Penguin Books.

Friedman, E, (1985). *Generation to Generation: Family Process in Church and Synagogue.* New York: Guilford Press.

..........*Holy Bible: New International Version* (1984). East Brunswick, NJ: International Bible Society.

Paloutzian, R. and Park, C. (eds.) (2005). *Handbook of the psychology of religion and spirituality.* New York: Guilford Press.

SUGGESTED READINGS

Briggs, W. (1991). *Transitions: Making the most of change.* Reading, MA: Wesley Publishing.

Crum, T. (1998). *The magic of conflict.* New York: Simon and Schuster.

Fisher, R. & Brown, S. (1988). *Getting together: Building relationships as we negotiate.* New York: Penguine Books.

CHAPTER IX
Putting It All Together

Any survey of counseling theories and techniques would probably leave the reader with many questions. One might ask for example, are there just a few theories and their practices that would be most helpful for the Christian counselor? Which theory best explains "what makes people tick"? What is required of the Christian counselor as a person in order to be an adequate vessel of the Holy Spirit? What specific abilities are shared by effective counselors regardless of their theoretical orientations? This concluding chapter will attempt to answer these important questions.

One way to "get a handle" on the variety of therapies that have been discussed is to put each of them in a category. That is, to cut the number of therapies from nine separate ones to two groups of therapies. The first group could be loosely called the talking therapies, the second group would be the teaching therapies.

The talking therapies include psychoanalysis, object relations and person-centered. They are called talking therapies because the practitioners believe that talking about oneself and one's problems can promote emotional well-being. These therapies require that the counselee does most of the talking while the counselor mostly listens. When working with a couple or a family, family systems would also be considered a talking therapy.

While the theories upon which the talking therapies are based could hardly be more diverse, the actual practice of each of them is very similar. The counselee talks about whatever he/she wants to talk about and the counselor responds in such a way as to increase his/her self-understanding.If the counselee is a couple or a family, then the counselor may be a little more involved in directing the counseling session but the goal is the same as it is for the other talking therapies. The couple or family will better understand how and why they interact with each other and the consequences of those interactions.

The talking therapies are normally long-term, sometimes sessions take place over many years. But their basic techniques can certainly be put to good use even when there is only one session, as the fictitious counseling sessions in previous chapters illustrated.

The second category of therapies is the teaching therapies. This category includes operant conditioning, classical conditioning, modeling and cognitive therapy. When working with a couple or a family, the counselor whose work is based on a structural theory would also be considered to be a teacher.

As the name of this category suggests, the counselee talks about his or her problem and then the counselor teaches the counselee how to over-come the problem. The teaching may include test-taking, role-play and homework assignments as well as assessments of the quality of the homework. With couples and families, structural family counseling uses the same techniques and adds some, like changing chairs during the counseling sessions.

The teaching therapies are short-term, typically lasting no more than two or three months of weekly, one-hour sessions. The counselor using these therapies is goal-directed and focused on a specific issue. [28]

Since the teaching therapies are so goal-directed, it is not surprising that they are not too interested in why there is a problem, only that there is one. That is, the teaching therapies do not deal with human motivation, with "what makes people tick."

---

[28] Those who use the talking therapies also establish goals with the counselee. But they would be long-term goals that would not be attainable for many months or even years. The non-professional counselor would not work that long with a counselee so specific goals may not be defined.

They are less concerned with what drives us, what motivates us than with how we actually behave, feel and think.

In fact, most of the theories that inform the teaching therapies assume that we don't even have any innate motivations. They believe that each individual is like a black box that simply waits to be filled by environmental influences. We learn to want something and that drives our behaviors and affects our emotions. Cognitive theory differs somewhat from the other teaching theories, however, in that it does suggest an innate motivation, which is to learn from and adapt to our environment.

While most of the learning theories are not interested in "what makes people tick," the theories that gave rise to the talking therapies are. But they each have a different answer to this fundamental question. Psychoanalysis assumes that sex and aggression are the primary motivating forces for all of human behavior. Object Relations Theory assumes that the motivation for the formation of personality is an innate need for relationships. The Rogerians (person-centered therapy) believe that we are motivated by the innate and future-oriented motivation to become self-actualized. As for the Christian understanding of "what makes people tick," that will be addressed in the biblical and theological reflections.

While the basic assumptions about motivation are different and often contradictory, the practitioners of all of the counseling theories do agree about the importance of certain abilities and attitudes of the counselor. These are (1) an ability to "connect" with another human being, (2) the ability to listen to the counselee and respond appropriately and (3) the capacity for empathy.

It just makes sense that if the counselor doesn't connect with the counselee, then the counselor's suggestions, prescriptions and interpretations may not get through - they will probably fall on deaf ears. Counseling without a connection between counselee and counselor would be like teaching hundreds of students who watch a professor's lecture on a television screen. The teacher may dispense pearls of real wisdom but one look at the students and it becomes clear that they are not interested. They may regurgitate the teacher's lecture when they are required to do so, but it has not made any lasting impact on them.

It is difficult to describe what it means to connect but we have all had experiences of either connecting or not connecting with another human being, so we know intuitively what that means. Sometimes we find it hard to connect to someone whom we've known for many years. Sometimes we have felt an instant connection with a complete stranger. We sensed from that stranger that he or she respected and cared about us so we felt connected. And that is the essence of the therapeutic relationship. Two (or more) people connect with each other because one of them genuinely cares about the other(s).

There is at least a potential for change, even in the briefest encounters, when the counselee recognizes that the counselor respects and cares about him or her. The counselor does not usually explicitly state this attitude of care and respect. But it is an attitude that most counselees will experience when it is present. Without the connection that happens when a counselee feels respected, accepted and cared about, the potential for change in the counselee is minimal.

There are, however, at least two impediments to forming a connection between a counselor and a counselee. The first is the counselor's own moral code and the second is a significant difference in the life experiences of the counselor and the counselee.

The Christian counselor has a moral code that is informed by scripture. He/she tries to live by that code. But not all Christians actually do live up to their own convictions about what is right and what is wrong. Some Christians drink too much. Others have adulterous affairs. Some Christians lie or steal or cheat. They may feel guilty about breaking their own code of morality but they do it anyhow.

Other Christians do live up to a scripture-based moral code. But that code may differ from a specific Christian counselor's code of morality. Some Christians believe that under certain circumstances it is all right to divorce, others have committed homosexual relationships, still others engage in pre-marital sex. Their biblically informed moral code does not consider these behaviors to be wrong.

When the Christian counselor seeks to minister to someone

who has different standards or a different code of morality from his own, that counselor needs to make a difficult decision. Can he relate to the counselee without being judgmental? Does he believe that the counselee's morality must be challenged even when that is not the person's agenda?

If the counselor cannot relate to an individual with respect for his or her differences, then that counselor must refer the counselee to someone who can. There can be no real connection when the counselor believes that he must convince a counselee that the counselor's own moral code or moral behavior is right and therefore the counselee's is wrong. Even if the counselor does not impose his moral code on the counselee, the counselor's judgmental attitude may be conveyed in subtle ways. In either case, the counselor is not likely to really connect with the counselee.

The second reason for a failure to connect with a counselee is that his or her life experiences seem completely alien to the counselor. Sometimes there are ethnic differences, sometimes there are socioeconomic differences between counselor and counselee. When these differences exist to the point at which two human beings cannot find their common humanity, then out of respect for the other, the counselor should refer the counselee to someone who shares a similar background with him or her.

It should be noted here, that "it takes two to tango" and this is also true in a counseling relationship. Sometimes it is the counselee who cannot overcome his/her differences from the counselor. When that happens, the counselee will probably find a different counselor without waiting for a referral. That is completely appropriate, even though it may be disappointing to the counselor. But as noted earlier, Christian ministry is not about our own needs and feelings. What is best for the counselee is the only thing that matters. If a particular counselee and a particular counselor cannot connect with each other, then a different counselor will better serve the counselee.

Effective counseling, then, requires an attitude of respect, acceptance and genuine caring for the counselee in order to form a connection, a therapeutic relationship. Effective counselors share another characteristic. They have the ability to really listen. Some counselors may need to be very intentional about saying very little in order to really listen, this is especially true when the counselee finds it difficult to speak. Listening well sometimes means exercising great patience during long silences. Listening well sometimes means expending real energy in order to focus on the counselee and ignore distractions.

A common distraction for many counselors is the memory of his or her own experiences that are similar to those of the counselee's. When the counselor finds himself thinking about his own experiences instead of the counselee's, it could be an indication that he is not listening very well. Of course, experiences that a counselor shares with a counselee will come to mind on occasion. But when the counselor's memories take his attention away from the counselee for more than the briefest period of time, then the counselor needs to be very intentional about re-focusing on listening to the counselee.[29]

While listening well is an important part of the counseling process, it is no less important to respond appropriately to what has been heard. Our responses to the counselee are, in the broadest sense of the word, interpretations. The type of interpretation, however, will differ according to the theoretical orientation of the individual counselor.

Generally speaking, the psychoanalytically oriented counselor will interpret unconscious material. The person-centered counselor will respond primarily to the counselee's feelings. The cognitive therapist will interpret the counselee's cognitive distortions and the person whose ministry is informed by any one of the three learning theories will use a technique (a type of interpretation) that can change the counselee's dysfunctional behavior or emotions. They may not call what they do interpretation, but all therapists engage in some kind of feedback about what they hear from the counselee.

When deciding what kind of interpretation to make, the

---

[29] There is a difference of opinion about whether or not the counselor should tell the counselee about shared experiences. It is the author's opinion that counselees are much more interested in their own lives than they are in the counselor's. So when the counselor tells the counselee about similar experiences it is usually just a distraction.

counselor needs to be cognizant of the fact that some types of interpretations work better than others depending on the individual counselee and the issue being addressed. An intelligent, insightful and highly verbal person will do well with the psychoanalytically informed therapies and with person-centered therapy. A person who finds it difficult to talk about emotions may be served better by a cognitive approach to counseling. Someone who only wants to deal with a specific issue may want to focus on that and not get sidetracked with "touchy feely stuff." In that case a teaching approach might work best. It is up to the counselor to adjust his/her interpretations to the person and the situation of the counselee.

Regardless of what theory or theories a counselor relies upon, there is one element of the therapeutic process that has been shown in study after study to be the hallmark of effective counseling. That is, the effective counselor is empathic (Korchin, 1976).

Empathy is the ability to feel what another is feeling. This requires that the counselor empty himself of his own feelings in order to experience the counselee's feelings. There are, however, two important issues that need to be noted about empathy.

First, some counselees are completely unaware of their own feelings. The empathic counselor may experience such a person's emotions but when he names them the counselee may deny that he/she is feeling anything. Fortunately, counselees who are incapable of recognizing their own emotions can be taught to do so.

The anxious person can see that she is anxious when the counselor points out that she is jiggling her foot and rapidly twisting a tissue. The counselor can then ask about the internal experience that the counselee is having. Can she feel her heart race, her muscles get tense, her breathing become shallow? If the counselee's face turns red and/or she starts to laugh for no apparent reason, then the counselor might suggest that she is embarrassed. The counselee who raises his voice can be asked to focus on what he feels, physiologically, when he is angry.

Feelings are an important part of the human experience. The person who is shut off from his/her own feelings is missing not only pain but the joy that might also be his/hers. The life of the person who does not recognize his/her own emotions is often filled with emptiness and apathy. Teaching such a person to recognize his/her own feelings can have a life-changing affect that is more than worth the effort.

The second issue regarding empathy is that the counselor needs to be both feeling and thinking. The counselor will be intentionally empathic for a time and then find it necessary to temporarily focus instead on thinking about what he/she is feeling. Is the counselor feeling what the counselee is feeling? If so, what is that feeling and why might the counselee be feeling that way? This is an internal process within the counselor. It requires a conscious effort to engage and disengage, to feel and then analyze those feelings.

The following example may help to illuminate this back and forth process of empathy and analysis. A group of college students gathers in a dormitory room to talk about their trips home during a recent break. One of the young men, we'll call him Tim, talks about his sister who has recently separated from her husband. He speaks in a matter-of-fact tone but is very critical of his sister because of the failure of her marriage. But Tim's best friend begins to feel profoundly sad and wonders why - she thinks about her sadness. The friend decides that she is actually empathizing with Tim's own sadness. She interrupts Tim and simply says "your sister's situation must make you pretty unhappy." And Tim breaks down in tears. He had been trying to hide from his own feelings for his sister by being critical of her. Tim's friend allowed him to express his genuine feelings, which in turn allowed the whole group to offer their support to Tim during this difficult time in his life.

These then are the attitudes and practices that the counselor uses regardless of his or her theoretical orientation; caring about and respecting the counselee in order to connect to another human being, listening without prejudice or distraction and responding to the counselee with both empathy and understanding.

While effective counselor's share similar attitudes and practices, nevertheless, every counselor is different. We each have our own unique strengths, weaknesses, experiences and circumstances. Some counselors are attuned to their own feelings, others take a more rational approach to life. The feeling person will need to concentrate on analyzing and the thinking person may need to be intentional about feeling what the counselee is feeling. Each Christian counselor is a human being who brings his or her own uniqueness to the counseling ministry.

This uniqueness must be acknowledged as well as treasured. That is, each counselor must be aware of who he or she is because it is *the person of the counselor that is so essential to effective counseling.* The counselor must know what are his or her special strengths as well as his or her own weaknesses. This is not to say that one's weaknesses cannot be ameliorated. But one must first be aware of his or her own weaknesses as well as his or her own strengths in order to be an adequate vessel of the Holy Spirit.

In addition to an honest self-appraisal of oneself, each individual counselor must also determine which theories and techniques provide the most useful framework on which to base his or her ministry. As previously noted, the particular theory that a counselor uses depends in large measure on the counselee to whom the counselor is ministering. So the best option is to know several theories and choose the best concepts and practices from each. That is, the effective counselor is usually eclectic.

All of the theories that have been presented have something to teach us. While it is clear that many of their assumptions and beliefs seem totally contradictory, that does not mean that there is no truth in these theories, even when they contradict each other. For example, psychodynamic theory cannot be more different from behaviorism. Psychoanalysts assume that people are driven by their animal instincts and behaviorists deny that we have any instincts at all. But these categorical statements can be understood as partly true and partly false. The fact is that psychoanalysts acknowledge that what we learn from our environments affects who we are and behaviorists understand that we do have physiological needs that motivate us - we need food, we need sleep and we are sometimes highly motivated to gratify our sexual appetites.

An eclectic approach accepts what is valid in each theory and ignores the rest. The eclectic counselor uses those techniques that are potentially useful and rejects those that are not. Eclecticism allows the counselor to learn more about how to minister effectively by comparing and contrasting theories and the different practices that come from these theories.

Most experienced counselors believe that an eclectic approach to counseling serves counselees better than one that is limited to a single theory. Having more than one way to minister to people who are all so different from each other seems far more desirable than the "cookie-cutter approach" of relying on only one theory.

There are, however, those counselors who choose to "fly by the seat of their pants." They would rather not use any theoretical understandings because none of them have been shown to be more reflective of reality or more widely useful than any other. Such a person chooses to use his own theory, even though he may describe himself as a practitioner without a theory.

There is much to be said for the person who chooses to be informed by his or her own understanding of human nature and who uses his or her own counseling techniques. On the positive side, a person who rejects all understandings but his own can be truly congruent [30] and therefore authentic. These are certainly good traits for any counselor. But the person who consciously rejects all theories but his own must also be aware of the limitations of his choice.

For example, a pastor decides that if he expresses his genuine love and acceptance for everyone who seeks his help, then people will benefit from his ministry. Without realizing it, that pastor is really a person-centered therapist who is limited to that one approach. In this case, the pastor who rejects all theories but his own has limited his ministry to those who are intelligent, verbally gifted, in touch with their own feelings and highly motivated to change. That leaves out a lot of people.

In addition to a theoretically eclectic approach, the Christian counselor must also be eclectic in terms of the techniques that he/she uses. The mostly widely used theories have produced various techniques that have, for decades, proven to be effective. They are not equally effective for all people, but knowing more than one technique allows the counselor to tailor his/her techniques

---

[30] Until the counselor has integrated a theory into his/her thinking, the "foreignness" of the theory prevents the highest degree of congruence.

to each individual counselee.

Sometimes counselors will be comfortable using just one specific technique. They assume that if a large number of people seek their counsel, then that one technique must be effective for everyone. For example, a counselor may use a technique that is designed to boost each counselee's self-esteem. The counselor may praise the counselee's accomplishments or motivations or attitudes or even his or her physical appearance. His technique is praising people and they do feel better as a result of his ministry.

Unfortunately, feeling better and experiencing healing are not the same thing. A person may feel better for a brief period of time, but that doesn't necessarily mean that any significant change has taken place in his or her life. Feeling better is not the same as healing. When a human being has experienced healing that usually means that he/she feels better because of a significant *change* in how he/she thinks and/or feels and/or behaves. It usually takes the ability to use several different techniques to promote real healing in individuals who are all so different from each other.

Of course, the healing power of the Holy Spirit is not necessarily thwarted by a limited number of techniques. But knowing and using several techniques probably makes us more usable vessels for a greater number of people.

In order to be a counselor who is able to offer the healing power of God to as many counselees as possible, it is highly recommended that he/she be eclectic, both in theoretical orientation and in the use of several different techniques. The following fictitious counseling session will demonstrate this eclectic approach.

Fictitious Counseling Session

Betsy is a woman in her mid-sixties who is the associate pastor of a large metropolitan church. She has been a widow for almost 11 years. She had three children, her son died in a car accident 17 years ago. The counselor is a professional pastoral counselor, certified by the American Association of Pastoral Counselors.

Line 1. Counselor: Hi, Betsy. Please come in.

Line 2. Betsy: Where would you like me to sit?

Line 3. Counselor (*taking a chair in front of his desk and pointing toward the chair opposite his own*): Why don't you try that one. *(Betsy takes a few minutes to get settled).* So, what brings you?

Line 4. Betsy: Well, to tell you the truth, I'm more than a little embarrassed about being here. I'm used to being the person other people tell their troubles to. But, here I am.

Line 5. Counselor: Here you are *(pause)*.

Line 6. Betsy: So, where should I start?

Line 7. Counselor: I don't know.

Line 8. Betsy: Well, I've been pretty down in the dumps lately, well, for quite a while. I don't know what's wrong. Well, that's not entirely true. I do know, I'm just too embarrassed to say it out loud *(pause)*. I have two daughters, they're both married, the one has two kids and the other has three. They're great kids. *(Smiling)* do you want to see their pictures?

Line 9. Counselor: Is this a delaying tactic?

Line 10. Betsy: Okay, here it comes *(crying)*. I have a good relationship with my older daughter, but the younger one, Denise, I just don't know what's going on with her. She lives about three hours away from me and I never see her. I know she's busy, but she never calls, she never sends a Mother's Day card or a birthday card. On the rare occasion when we do have lunch together she acts like she can hardly wait to get away. She eats her lunch and poof, she's gone.

Line 11. Counselor: That hurts.

Line 12. Betsy: The problem is, Denise resents me because when her brother died I was not there for her. I know she's mad at me about it - but that was seventeen years ago.

Line 13. Counselor: How do you know she's mad at you? Have you asked her?

Line 14. Betsy: Well, no. You mean that's not why she's mad at me?

Line 15. Counselor: You see, you're making two mistakes here. You assume that she's mad at you and you believe that you can read her mind. Maybe there are other explanations for her

[220]

behavior. Is she super busy, is her job stressful, are her kids giving her grief? And even if she is mad at you, we certainly don't why she is.

Line 16. Betsy: I see what you're saying. Maybe she isn't mad at me, maybe she's mad at someone else, maybe she isn't mad at all, maybe she's just really stressed out. And you're right, even if she is mad at me, I really can't read her mind.

Line 17. Counselor: Way to go, Betsy. Good for you. You've realized that you shouldn't make assumptions and that you're not a mind reader. So, have you tried talking to Denise, asking her if there is a problem between the two of you?

Line 18. Betsy: Oh no, I couldn't do that. She'd have a fit. I just couldn't stand it.

Line 19. Counselor: It would absolutely mean the end of the world, that the earth would no longer revolve around the sun if you tried to talk to her.

Line 20. Betsy: Well, it feels like it would be the end of the world.

Line 21. Counselor: It *feels* scary, but you *believe* it would be unbearable.

Line 22. Betsy: Yeah, how I feel doesn't make it true. *(Long pause).* I wish I could get over this. Why am I torturing myself like this? It really isn't the end of the world even if she is mad at me. I know I love her, even though she doesn't seem to know that way deep down she loves me. I know that as long as I love her that our relationship will never be broken. Maybe some day she'll realize that she loves me too - and act like it. I have to think more about what I need to do in order to be who I want to be and less about how I want other people to treat me.

Analysis

Lines 1-3. The counselor would have alleviated some of Betsy's anxiety by suggesting which chair to take as soon as Betsy came in the room. Being a good host is a sign of respect for the person who is visiting the counselor's office and it begins the session in a caring way.

Line 4. Betsy gives the counselor a great deal of information from the very start. First, she is very much aware of her own feelings of anxiety and does not hesitate to make them known to a complete stranger. She is also insightful about herself, she knows that at least part of her discomfort is due to a reversal of roles. Betsy is more comfortable being the counselor than the counselee. That is, she is aware of her own feelings and has good insight about herself. She has the characteristics of a relatively healthy person who is having a difficult time resolving a very specific issue.

Line 5. The counselor invites Betsy to say whatever she wants to say without suggesting any particular topic or way to proceed. This is typical of person-centered counselors. Psychoanalytically informed counselors may have instructed Betsy to just say whatever comes into her mind without thinking about it before she speaks.

Line 6. The psychoanalytically informed counselor would also take note of what Betsy unconsciously reveals about herself. First, when in a new situation she becomes unsure of herself. Also, she looks for help when she's feeling vulnerable. She does not need to pretend to herself or the counselor that she is completely self-sufficient. This too is a good sign that there is real potential that counseling will have a positive outcome. If Betsy felt that she had to maintain a façade of invulnerability, then she would be much less responsive to the counselor's input.

Line 7. This particular response would be typical of a person-centered counselor. It is an honest statement about his own ignorance. It also "puts the ball in Betsy's court" as it emphasizes that she is responsible for herself and must make her own decisions.

Line 8. Once Betsy is given free rein to talk about whatever she chooses to talk about, she is forthcoming (but embarrassed) about her problem. Then she hides her embarrassment through the use of humor when she offers to show the counselor pictures of her grandchildren. Actually, humor is an excellent coping mechanism when one is anxious or embarrassed and shows that Betsy has the maturity to laugh at herself without being self-deprecating.

Line 9. The counselor recognizes that Betsy was joking when

she offered to show him pictures of her grandchildren. He can be mildly confrontational about her offer because he senses that she is strong enough to do well with confrontation. It also shows a high degree of congruity on the counselor's part. His response was honest and straightforward.

The psychoanalytically informed counselor would have acknowledged Betsy's resistance. He might have said something like "you are not very comfortable talking about what's bothering you."

Line 10. At last Betsy is comfortable enough to expose her emotions as well as a problem that is difficult for her. One might guess that Betsy is aware that a troubled relationship with her daughter might be interpreted as Betsy's failure as a mother and that this awareness would certainly cause her some embarrassment (line 8).

Line 11. The counselor's empathic response would be typical of all of the talking therapies. He doesn't say that Betsy alone is hurting, he implies that he shares her hurt.

Line 12. Betsy talks about her perceived failure as a mother. Apparently she believes that if she knew what Denise was angry about that somehow it would help her to repair her relationship with her daughter.

Line 13. The counselor could have taken one of two directions. He might have interpreted Betsy's unstated belief that she is a failure as a mother (the psychoanalytically oriented approach) or he could take a cognitive approach and challenge Betsy's cognitive distortions. He may have chosen the latter course because he recognizes that Betsy is an emotionally healthy person who does not require in-depth counseling. She wants to deal with a specific issue, and that is often best accomplished by using cognitive therapy.

Line 14. The counselor's interpretation seems to take Betsy by surprise. She has probably been so convinced that she was a terrible mother that the idea that something else might explain her troubled relationship with her daughter seems completely foreign to her.

Line 15. Now the counselor explains Betsy's cognitive distortions. Betsy treats her assumption (that Denise is angry with her) as a fact, one that the counselor challenges. In addition, Betsy thinks that she can read her daughter's mind, that she knows why her daughter is angry with her.

Line 16. Betsy seems almost relieved at the counselor's interpretations of her own cognitive distortions. His decision to use cognitive therapy seems to have been a good one. The counselor could have also used a more psychoanalytically informed approach.

The death of a child is always such a traumatic event that most parents never fully recover from the loss. A psychoanalytically oriented counselor might pursue the possibility that Betsy was angry with her son for dying (a very common experience). Was Betsy projecting her own grief-related anger on to her daughter? That is, at an unconscious level, did Betsy assume that Denise was angry with her when it was actually Betsy's own anger that she attributed to her daughter? But the counselor trusted his own capacity for empathy. He did not experience anger from Betsy (which he probably would have if she used the defense mechanism of projection) so he stayed with a cognitive approach.

Line 17. The counselor uses the technique of positive reinforcement that comes from operant conditioning. His response will, theoretically at least, increase the probability that Betsy will remember her own cognitive distortions and avoid falling prey to them again.

At this point the counselor could have suggested family counseling for Betsy and Denise. He decided not to do that for two reasons. First, Denise lives too far away. Second, by resolving Betsy's cognitive distortions, the relationship between Betsy and her daughter will change considerably. When one person in the relationship changes, the other one will respond and over time will also make some changes.

Line 18. Betsy reveals another cognitive distortion - catastrophic thinking.

Line 19. The counselor uses a paradoxical intervention. He grossly exaggerates Betsy's fears.

Line 20. Another cognitive distortion. This one is the failure to differentiate between thoughts and feelings.

Line 21. The counselor trusts Betsy's motivation to change and the power of God in her life to effect that change. So his explanation is short and to the point.

Line 22. Betsy's fears about her daughter's anger have been alleviated. Now she is able to take a different perspective. She draws on her belief that the essence of the gospel is to love God, self and neighbor. As a result she comes to a conclusion that sounds like a continuation toward self-actualization.

Betsy's conclusion is significant because it sounds like person-centered therapy. But person-centered counseling was not the main theory used by the counselor. When a counselee uses language that comes from the counselor's theoretical leanings, then there is reason to fear that the counselee is simply modeling the counselor. Since Betsy does not use the counselor's language, the counselor can be assured that he did not exercise undue influence over the counselee. Betsy maintained her own uniqueness.

Biblical and Theological Reflections

Earlier in this chapter, assumptions about "what makes people tick" were discussed. The reader discovered that, among the major theories, there is no agreement at all about the answer to this question. But the answer is important to the counseling ministry. If we don't know what motivates people, then we can't really understand our counselees any more than we can really understand ourselves. Nor can we know what drives people to want to change when change is clearly required if a human being is to move from suffering to triumph. Psychological theories obviously do not give us the answer to the question "what makes people tick." Fortunately, the Bible does.

Christians will sometimes read the Bible in search of the answer to the question "what motivates us to be who we are?" And each biblical scholar will probably come away with a different answer. The following discourse is the author's answer to this important question. The reader is encouraged to find his or her own biblically informed answer.

We read in the first verse of the Bible "in the beginning God created..." (Genesis 1:1). When God created the universe, He also created human beings. Why? So that God might have a relationship with us and we might have a relationship with God (Teilhard de Chardin, 1955). As Object Relations Theory suggests, it is in meeting our innate need (*i.e.,* motivation) to relate that we define who we are. But as Christians we can go a step farther, our need to relate to God is our very reason for being.

The entire Bible is the story of humanity's relationship with God. Sometimes that relationship is seen through God's interactions with one person (*e.g.,* Noah, Abraham, Moses). Sometimes humanity's relationship with God is exemplified by His interactions with a nation (Israel) or the Church.

All of scripture is the story of a relationship between God and humanity. A relationship that cannot be broken. Despite sin, despite disobedience, despite the crucifixion, God has never given up on us. God continues to relate to humanity because of who God is. God is love. But that relationship between God and humanity is a two-way street. Human beings also seek to relate to God because apart from that relationship life is not only without purpose, it is meaningless.

It is because we have this need to have a relationship with God that the two main themes of this book have been repeated so often. The first oft-repeated theme is that we must love God, our neighbor and ourselves. That is the essence of what it means to have a relationship. To love God is not a feeling, it is an attitude. It is a recognition of our bond, our connection with God and His creation. It is this bond that we value more highly than anything else in our lives.

The second theme of this book is the need to forgive our neighbors. When we do not forgive, the connection between self and other is broken. When we fail to forgive, the commandment to love our neighbors is disobeyedWhen we do not love because we do not forgive we have destroyed our reason for being - the reason we were created in the first place.

The Jewish philosopher, Martin Buber, has beautifully addressed the human need to relate to others including to God. He wrote "Extended, the lines of relationship intersect in the eternal You" (Buber, 1970, p. 123). That is, when we love ourselves we are also loving God. When we love our neighbors, our communities, all of God's creation, we love the omnipresent Creator who both transcends His creation and is present in it.

So, in answer to the question, what makes us tick, what is the primary motivation in the development of each human being's unique personality, the author suggests that it is to love ourselves, our neighbors, our world and the God who created it all so that He might relate to us and we might relate to Him.

Questions to Consider

1) Name the practices that are common to all of the theories that have been presented.

2) Compare and contrast Object Relations Theory and practice with behaviorism's theory and practice.

3) Compare and contrast Person-Centered Theory and practice with Cognitive Theory and practice.

4) If you choose to work according to your own understanding of human beings, what specifically is that understanding? What is the authority for your theory? Does your style of counseling come from your theory? Be specific in showing how your understandings inform your counseling.

5) Are you an empathic listener? Give three examples of conversations in which that characteristic was evident.

6) What does your understanding of scripture teach you about "what makes us tick."

REFERENCES

Buber, M., W. Kaufmann (trans.) (1970). *I and You.* New York: Scribner's Sons.

..........*Holy Bible: New International Version* (1984). East Brunswick, NJ: International Bible Society.

Korchin, S. (1976). *Modern clinical psychology: Principles of intervention in the clinic and community.* New York: Basic Books.

Teilhard de Chardin, P., (1955). *The phenomenon of man.* New York: Harper and Row.

SUGGESTED READING

Norcross, J. & Goldfried, M (eds.) (1992). *Handbook of integrative psychotherapy.* New York: Basic Books.

Teilhard de Chardin, P., (1955). *The phenomenon of man.* New York: Harper and Row.

Subject Index

acceptance 71, 80, 110, 213, 218

anger 7, 12, 19-21, 23-4, 27, 29, 44-6, 49, 60, 63, 78-9, 86, 93, 117, 132, 135, 142-5, 150, 167-9, 178, 186-9, 193-4, 196, 204, 212, 222, 224-5

anxiety 24, 28, 39, 41, 53, 79, 102-4, 108, 128, 169-70, 179, 196, 221-2

assumptions 22, 69, 73, 81, 84, 105, 113, 115, 211, 217, 221, 225

autism, normal 39, 47, 63-4, 66

autonomy 53-4, 163, 167-8

awareness 18-20, 38-9, 71, 136, 169, 223

behaviorists 15, 90, 97, 217

behaviors 7, 24-5, 64, 77-8, 89-90, 92, 96, 99, 107, 113-4, 116-7, 120-1, 126-7, 134, 168, 174, 211-2

boundaries 27, 162, 166, 168

Christian counselor 1-3, 8-12, 14-5, 17, 22, 30-1, 35, 42, 45-6, 54, 63-5, 77, 81-2, 84, 94-6, 106, 108-9, 115, 121, 124, 126-7, 131, 133, 138, 146, 153, 156-7, 181, 185, 209, 212, 217-8

classical conditioning 90, 92-5, 100, 103, 108, 110, 210

cognitive 31, 52, 110, 113-22, 124-9, 192-3, 195, 200, 204, 210-1, 214-5, 223-4, 227

distortion 118, 125, 128, 214, 223

confrontation 125, 144, 150, 171, 179, 194, 204, 223

congruence 72, 80-1, 85, 106, 218

development 11, 14, 16, 35, 38, 44-7, 52-4, 56, 63-8, 70, 87, 95, 114, 117, 127-9, 163, 167, 196, 227 dysfunctional 10, 40, 42, 53, 72, 86, 132, 134, 142-4, 155-7, 163, 174, 178-82, 214

empathy 79, 80, 125, 125, 211, 215-6

faith 3, 5, 9, 11-2, 14-5, 104, 108, 115, 124, 126, 151, 154, 156,

family 5, 9, 14, 60, 82, 137, 139-40, 151, 158-9, 161-80, 182-3, 206, 209-10, 224

forgive 14, 30, 120, 126-7, 133, 144, 149-50, 196-7, 200, 226

goals 9, 86, 89, 115, 133-4, 137, 144, 210

God 11, 14-6, 22, 43, 45-7, 51-4, 64-5, 75-6, 81, 84-5, 106-8, 126-7, 153-4, 181, 190, 196-7, 205, 219, 225-6

happiness 8, 44, 48, 61, 119, 153, 170, 174, 179-81

Holy Spirit 12-5, 22, 30-1, 85, 127, 209, 217, 219

homework 120-2, 176, 179, 210, 220

insight 2, 20, 23, 27, 61-2, 64, 73, 81, 120

interpretation 17, 23-5, 29, 37, 44, 59, 77, 80, 89, 98, 126-7, 134-5, 142, 171, 187, 206, 211, 214-5, 223-4

Jesus 11, 13, 62, 64, 66, 82, 102-3, 107-8, 181, 196-7

love 12-14, 18, 21, 26, 29-30, 36-8, 41, 43, 46-8, 55-7, 61, 63, 65, 71, 76, 81, 85-6, 133-4, 139, 145, 150, 152-3, 170, 181, 191, 194, 206, 218, 221, 225-7

maturity 11, 19, 44, 54, 60, 167, 222

mental representation 37-8, 40, 54, 56-7, 61, 63

motivation 18-9, 22, 35, 59, 63, 70, 90, 92, 144, 173, 179, 210-1, 219, 225-7

personality 2, 7, 35, 42, 64-7, 69, 73, 85, 105, 171, 197, 205, 211, 227

positive reinforcement 90-1, 94-5, 98-100, 106-7, 109, 110, 126, 224

power 5-6, 8, 10-1, 13-6, 22, 38, 57, 78, 80, 85, 91, 93, 98-9, 106-9, 132, 134, 136-9, 143-4, 147, 149-51, 155-7, 161-2, 167-8, 174-9, 181, 185, 187-8, 190-1, 196, 199, 200, 203-5, 219, 225

presence 9, 15, 46, 56, 63 92, 102, 126, 150

punishment 21, 60

resistance 17, 24-5, 27-8, 32, 140, 180, 223

roadblocks 8, 13-5, 22, 54, 139, 196-7

schemata 117-8, 127

self-actualization 70, 72-4, 80-4, 86, 89, 163, 225

self-defeating 2, 10, 14, 22, 36, 56, 120, 122, 124, 127
structural 171, 174, 177, 179-80, 182, 210
subjective 37, 41, 71, 116, 128
therapeutic 2, 3, 11, 16, 33, 36, 59, 70 73, 86, 103, 113, 139, 144,
      181
transference 17, 20-2, 25, 32, 50, 60

CPSIA information can be obtained
at www.ICGtesting.com
Printed in the USA
LVHW091456170321
681760LV00025B/157

9 781432 738617